FIGURE IT OUT

HOW TO HARNESS THE POWER OF RESOURCEFULNESS AND ACHIEVE SUCCESS

KATE MEINER

Figure It Out: How to Harness the Power of Resourcefulness and Achieve Success

Copyright © 2019 by Kate Meiner

All rights reserved.

ISBN: 978-1-7343929-1-3

No part of this publication may be reproduced, distributed, or transmitted in any form, by any means, including photocopying, recording, or other electronic or mechanical methods, without the prior written permission of the publisher, except in the case of brief quotations embodied in critical reviews and certain other noncommercial uses permitted by copyright law.

Disclaimer: Names and identifying details have been changed to protect the privacy of individuals.

Cover creation courtesy of Firlie Fadilah

Editing and formatting by Lorraine Reguly from www.WordingWell.com

FIGURE IT OUT

Dedication

To my unwavering support system—thank you for always being there for me.

FIGURE IT OUT

"It's not a lack of resources, it's your lack of resourcefulness that stops you."

—TONY ROBBINS

Table of Contents

Note from the Author	9
Intro: The Greatest Skill You Can Learn	13
Part 1: LEARNING: The Foundation	17
Chapter 1: Mindset	19
Chapter 2: Habits	37
Chapter 3: The Realm of Possibilities	51
Part 2: BEING: Building the Skill Sets of the Resourceful	65
Chapter 4: Problem Solving—Being a Problem-Solver	67
Chapter 5: Learning and Curiosity—Being Learning-Based	75
Chapter 6: Adaptability—Being Adaptive	85
Chapter 7: Observance—Being Observant	93
Chapter 8: Creativity—Being Creative	105
Chapter 9: Productivity—Being Productive	111
Part 3: IMPLEMENTING: Taking MASSIVE Action	123

Chapter 10: Ask Powerful Questions	127
Chapter 11: "No Dead End" Mentality	135
Chapter 12: Grit and Determination	145
Chapter 13: Discipline	155
Chapter 14: Find Inspiration	161
Chapter 15: Get a Coach	165
Part 4: CONCLUSION—Figuring it Out!	171
Questions for You	174
Recommended Reads	177
Coaching Tools and Resources	181
Acknowledgements	182
About the Author	185

Note from the Author

If you were asked what the greatest skill set to have is, what would your response be? What if someone was curious to know the best tool at one's disposal—what do you think it is?

The reality is, we all possess many important skills. You likely have lots of attributes that are recognized among your peers as impressive talents, and you probably really have a knack for something that seems to come easily to you but that others struggle with. There are many great skills to have and easy to explain on a job resume—an extensive list of personal strengths such as good communicator, fast learner, proficient in Word, dependable, punctual, organized, efficient—the list goes on and on, with great qualities that each of us know to be our strengths and would benefit us and others.

But what if I told you that there is one skill set, one word, the Mac Daddy of talent that would trump them all? Wouldn't you want to know what it is, how to use it, and how to become a person who possesses such a skill or talent? Well, you're in luck! That's exactly what this book is designed to do! It will explain the value of being resourceful and help you become a more resourceful person. Believe me, everyone is capable of harnessing resourcefulness. There is a way to learn, too! You can learn to think differently, you can learn to lead people, you can learn to provide more value, and by doing so, make an impact much greater than you ever thought possible. You can create a life of opportunities, discover the power of being resourceful, and see the impact it can have on your life. You can learn to master this powerful trait that will empower you with a set of skills that will serve you for a lifetime. It's ALL possible. Any reality you choose to experience can be yours!

What makes people successful? What skill is it that allows people to achieve great levels of success? These questions can be answered by knowing and understanding the importance of learning to be resourceful. In this book, I'm going to lay out the most important and key element to success: resourcefulness.

By sheer definition, resourcefulness is having the ability to find quick and clever ways to overcome difficulties. Now, I don't know about you, but I most definitely have faced my fair share of difficulties. We are all faced with challenges and adversities, and we will forever be continuously faced with them. The problem is that most people throw the towel in, saying, "It can't be done," or "There's no way out." People tend to give in or give up because it's just easier. It's easier than solving a problem. It's easier than being creative. It's also easier for them because they aren't resourceful. If you are a resourceful person, success tends to come more naturally. That's right, not more *easily;* the key word here is more *naturally*. You start to see possibilities that others can't dare to see. And in this roller coaster we are on called life, the ups and downs will certainly come and go.

You will have setbacks, but being able to deal with those setbacks or those challenges will serve you a heck of a lot better if you are resourceful. Resourceful people tend to have a lot of determination and grit, so they tend to have lots of life experiences that led to more abundance. And that's what I want for you! I want you to have lots of abundance, options, and opportunities. I want you to find a solution, whatever the situation, whatever the circumstances, or whatever the roadblock. You will be able to "figure it out."

Resourcefulness is the key to becoming successful, allowing you to change, adapt, think creatively, and problem-solve. It's the missing piece most look for, yet never find. If others would shift their attention from trying to become successful to becoming resourceful, then success is certainly bound to show up. All of the resources are around you, and in this book, you will learn to find those resources, harness their talents, and use them to achieve success.

So, what does it take in order to become successful? Your ability to become resourceful!

-Kate

Introduction:

The Greatest Skill You Can Learn

I'm so excited you're embarking on the inspiring road to achieve more, be more, and succeed at a higher level!

In this book, you will journey through three major sections.

One is the foundation for learning, where we will do a deep dive into understanding the power of our thoughts and how they can dramatically influence what actions we take.

The second section introduces you to the most important skill set you could ever learn, which is how to be more resourceful. Resourceful people have some unique abilities that catapult them to success. Most other books—and I've read countless of business, personal development, mindset, financial, and success books—don't mention the idea or concept of how one's level of resourcefulness is the key to success. Most of the books out there today touch on all the other traits and skills like self-awareness, grit, your ability to influence, habits, goal-setting, thinking big, and leadership.

Yet, what I've discovered is that all those skills become easier to gain or sharpen when you have the foundational piece of resourcefulness.

I hope you discover that, too. (*Be sure to check out my list of book recommendations in the back.*)

Thirdly, in the last section, you will bring those first two sections into action and implementation. Implement so that you continue to build on your experiences to achieve success, because this section is all about taking action toward your goals. I'm going to give a lot of examples and silly analogies (I'm preparing you now for some cheesy stories and comments, so just go with it!) in order to help you to relate and connect the dots in your own life as well as give you some things to work on after you complete this book.

There's nothing worse than reading an amazing book or taking an incredible class and then changing nothing with your actions—or inactions.

You might notice that all the sections end in "ING." Flash back to all those moments when you played

FIGURE IT OUT

Mad Libs as a kid, when it asked for verbs ending in "ING." My purpose in doing so is this: "ING" verbs show the present tense, that you're currently doing the action or activity, verses saying you will in the future, or that you've "been there, done that" before, in the past.

Action is all about being present. This entire book is designed to keep you in the present because the only place you can grow and develop is right now, in the moment! It's all here, waiting for you to take action and change your destiny!

Let's get started!

Part 1: LEARNING—The Foundation

In this section, we will focus on the power of your thoughts and your mindset. Everything begins here—everything! Mindsets shape the lives we lead, the actions we take, and the future possibilities of the world we live in.

Your thoughts and the power of your mind can be your biggest surge to your success or the biggest limitation that holds you back. Therefore, you must choose wisely and make the decision that it will be your surge; that your mindset will be focused on who you want to become and what you desire to achieve.

Your thoughts, words, experiences, and actions create the mindset in which you approach your life and how you see your potential future, so it's important that you know how to control your thoughts and harness the power of your mind.

1

Mindset

"Your thoughts determine what you do, and what you do determines who you are."

—*UNKNOWN*

Everything begins with your mindset. How you think and the level of focus of your thoughts will determine 90% of the results that you desire. Therefore, it is your mindset that we need to begin with, for you will only have the success and the results that match your level of thinking.

Every thought has power. Your thoughts have the power to form your beliefs, to form your reactions to the challenges you face, and to form the confidence you need. Everything you experience stems from your thoughts. It all starts with you.

In order to take away the key elements you need to meet your potential and achieve success, you must start with you.

Who are you? What are your most valued characteristics? What are you working toward? Who do you choose to be in the future?

These are some heavy questions, I'm sure, but they are critical for you to understand so that you will be able to take away the most value from this book.

I want to demonstrate something with an example. Say you decide to take a road trip to the beach. Great! You pack up a few towels, a cooler, some sunscreen, and a few snacks. You're excited and ready to go. All that's left now is for you to hop in the car and go, except you haven't yet decided which beach you will go to. If you live in Florida (like I do), where there is no shortage of beaches to take a road trip to, you will have very different experiences at each beach destination, depending on which one you choose.

Let's narrow down the choices. Should you head toward the Atlantic Ocean or the Gulf Coast? It depends on what you wish to experience. If you're looking to go surfing, you won't find many good waves on the Gulf. If you're looking for white sand, your chances are higher on the Gulf than near the Atlantic. The entire coastline is beach after beach after beach, each offering a slightly different experience. So, what does it matter? All you want is some sun and an ocean—that's the beauty of traveling to the beach. What else do you really need? If you see some dolphins or manatees, that would be cool, but that's not why you're going to the beach. If you were looking for seashells to collect, that would be fun—you could take a stroll and find some shells—but if you go home without them, no biggie.

Both seem like great beach trips, right? But why leave that to chance? You could decide the exact experience in advance if you knew what you wanted and how you would get there. My point in using this beach trip analogy is to see how many of you are currently treating life like an unplanned beach road trip.

It doesn't really matter what you do for an occupation or if you enjoy it or not, if you can pay your bills. Isn't that why you have a job anyway? It doesn't matter what stores you shop at; they all have the same stuff. All your friends don't really impact anything; they are just fun to be around.

Can you see how *not* understanding yourself, who you are, and what's important to you can shift you into operating on autopilot, so it's like you are just driving in any direction, hoping to hit a beach?

It's important to have a clear idea of who you are and who you want to be. In the absence of a clear destination, you'll take any route, and you'll end up at any beach. It won't matter which road you're on or where you end up. Now, I'm sure those adventurous souls out there love this idea of unplanned spontaneity, for I am one of those wanderlust travelers. However, when it comes to my life, my purpose, and how I spend my time, to just wing those types of things sounds awful. Life is so much more precious than that! Don't take just any route or go to just any old beach, because that's setting yourself up to live and be average, embarking on a mediocre road trip. When you're going through life on autopilot, where everything's average or mediocre, you're not meeting your potential. That's not what you were made for.

You have so much more inside of you, so you shouldn't dare settle for just any route, to end up at any beach. This and every trip should be the road trip of a lifetime, with your favorite people, to the best beach, having the greatest experiences. But that's not what most of us do, so I'm here to show you a way that you can break through mediocrity and meet your potential by achieving success through harnessing the power of resourcefulness.

In order to do this, it's important to know who you are and why you are moving forward. In order to accomplish that, you must take a deep look inside, at your thoughts and beliefs. Success isn't a skill set; it's a mindset. Your thoughts set the tone and predict what your body will do in response to the thoughts your brain is having. So, it is of the utmost importance that we begin with your mindset.

The mind is a powerful tool and it's important to know how it can help create the future of your dreams or completely sabotage your every move. Your mind is there to protect you, going all the way back to ancient times, where men wore fur and hunted wooly mammoths in the freezing ice.

Our brains were created to keep us safe from dangerous situations, which is a wonderful, great, amazing thing, except for the fact that we no longer live in such a survivor state anymore—at least, not the life-or-death battle every day, the moment you step outside your front door, fearing that you might be eaten by something. Our brains do a good job of collecting data to know what will bring harm and what will keep us safe, which is normally a good thing. At the same time, though, our brain can be so focused on keeping us safe that it holds us back from many other great, amazing things.

The brain is a powerful tool. It is complex, in many ways. It also doesn't know the difference between what's real and what's imaginary.

To think that some of the world's greatest minds struggle with knowing what is real or what's true is a fascinating concept. I actually learned this in an article I read, and it all has something to do with neuroscience. Now, I can assure you, I haven't studied many science-related fields—I was actually an art major in college—but I am an avid reader and do my research all the time.

In one particular case study, volunteers were asked to play a simple sequence of piano notes each day for five consecutive days. Another set of volunteers were asked to simply imagine themselves playing the notes. They were seated at the piano and visualized themselves playing the notes without actually playing anything. Both sets of volunteers then had their brains scanned—specifically, the region of the brain that is connected to the finger muscles. Believe it or not, those scans came out identical, proving that our brain couldn't tell the difference between those who actually played the piano and those who just simply imagined that they did. This is why athletes will tell you their game is 90% mental and 10% skill and training. This is why patients who visualize the healing process truly do recover faster.

This is why, when you set a goal and you picture yourself already achieving that goal, you are more likely to actually achieve it! Now, that's pretty neat. This proves that you can harness the power of your thoughts to create the life you truly desire, the life you are capable of living. So, if your brain doesn't know you're not successful, you should act—every day— as if you already are. If you do that, your mind will start to believe those thoughts, and those thoughts will begin to be the truth, that will shape your current reality.

We must stay in control of this powerful tool called our mindset because it's almost as if, in our current reality, our brain can be playing tricks on us. Although it is capable of many extraordinary things, the brain's number one, sole focus is to keep us safe and harm-free. Therefore, at times, our brain can hold us back from taking a good or necessary risk. It can convince us that to leave a job or a mediocre relationship is wrong and crazy, that bad things will happen to us, or we will be in pain if we attempt to do one of these so-called irrational things. So, we, being humans who listen to that powerful, convincing voice in our heads, stay put. We stay complacent and mediocre, going through the boring, monotonous, day-to-day routines, simply because our brains are content in us doing so. It is what is safe and comfortable, for the brain.

If you are to combat those thoughts and that hard-wired idea to remain comfortable, to break-free from the ordinary, you must know this underlying principle: you must understand your mindset and how you can choose to override all those thoughts and block those voices of doubt. You—the ambitious go-getter—know that what truly lies on the other side of that dark, scary abyss is a great adventure, a world of possibilities, and a life that you've never experienced.

It is one thing to know and understand the thoughts you have in your mind but it's another to understand the positive and negative effects those thoughts have on your life. Here's another idea that should give you a bout of confidence that this notion of achieving success will be simple (that was sarcasm; it won't be simple): your mind will default to thinking negative thoughts first, and it will binge-watch negative thoughts, negative reactions, and all those "what ifs" over and over and over again.

This is why most people tend to be worrywarts in life; it's simply your brain's way to caution you and ultimately convince you NOT to take risks or pursue your passions.

Did you know that in the English language there are approximately 200 words associated with positivity and around 700 associated with negativity? That's over triple the amount of negative words we know and use in our society over positive ones! It's no wonder we lead our lives being scared and just dream about achieving success one day!

The second underlying principle you must know and understand on your resourceful success journey: you will continually be faced with negative beliefs and thoughts. They won't ever go away. Some will be your own, and many will be from others. The ones that are your own most likely stemmed from someone else who instilled those negative thoughts and ideas in you. It's important that you are armed and ready to discard and reject these negative, "normal" notions and be able to rewire your brain from those embedded in you at a young age from others. That way, you can eventually build up the courage to go for it and open your yoga studio, start an online business, go back to school, study the culinary arts, or pursue any of your passions!

When you make the decision to go for it, the moment after you decide to take that action, your brain will start convincing you of all the reasons why you shouldn't do it and why you shouldn't continue taking an incredible, massive action toward a better you. This is the sabotaging part of your brain. It will ALWAYS be a struggle to overcome those first negative thoughts, to continue to battle with them, day in and day out—the first thoughts that tell you you're a loser, that you're going to fail, it won't pan out, you'll lose all your money, you'll lose your job, etc.

It is those moments when your mindset will be tested. That is precisely why you must remain focused on the future and focused on what lies beyond the negative thoughts.

You need to stay focused on the new, amazing life that you will be living when it does work. You need to stay focused on the freedom, the happiness, the wealth, the relationships, and the health you are then going to be experiencing because of your new mindset. How do you do that? Of course, it doesn't just happen that easily. When you wake up and decide that you and your future will look differently today, it's important to then anchor that commitment to an enormous *why*—to a sense of purpose, something bigger than you. Otherwise, you will find your journey to be very short-lived and your life will be the exact same as you have lived it thus far.

If you have a dream of pursuing a passion or a business idea, you must have a clear understanding of why you desire to achieve it.

Simply wanting to, or saying "I don't know, I just thought it'd be cool or it seems like it's a great idea" is the kind of thinking that won't make it through the battlefield of self-doubt and negative judgments or opinions. Having your *why* defined clearly is incredibly important because everything and everyone, throughout your resourcefulness journey, will tell you your idea is not a good idea. Therefore, you're why, what's speaking to you in your heart, is the purpose for why you desire the change. That *why* will be your only supporter; your lifeline to reach out to when you feel stuck, lost, or defeated.

FIGURE IT OUT

You must keep your focus on that why and the new and better end results. You must keep your focus on how your life will look completely different in the end.

John D Rockefeller once said, "Don't be afraid to give up the good to go for the great." These are very wise words to remember; to not to settle for just "good enough" when greatness is inside of us. It sounds simple, right? Sounds easy enough? Well, if that were true, then everyone would be fulfilled and happy. In actuality, the great is achieved by only a few, whose life's purpose was actually carried out. Not having clarity is the reason why many people don't reach the finish line. There are a bunch waiting at the starting line, yet so few finish. Finishing will be one of the most difficult challenges you face, because of the nature of our minds.

In order to help you succeed on your path to learning the great skill of resourcefulness, I've laid out a few simple solutions to help you get over the fear of wondering if you're good enough. The fear of self-doubt will continue to show up throughout your life in many capacities. No matter the situation or where you are in your process, you will need to reject all those limiting beliefs, ignore all the negative inner voices, and disregard all the bad advice you get from so-called friends and family who try and convince you that whatever your passion is, is a horrible idea.

There are a few great ways to help you get prepared to meet your potential. I can say this with confidence because there are many people who have literally written books on these topics. These are things that work best to help in overcoming such limiting beliefs and beating all those negative views and damaged judgments that run consistently through our minds. Be sure to write all these down!

Affirmations

The first one, and quite possibly the most powerful is affirmations. Positive affirmations are powerful statements that are repeated on a daily basis that will rewire your brain from thinking bad thoughts to thinking and believing powerful good ones. Affirmations are also defined as the action or process of affirming something, which implies that yes, you must take action on your affirmations and truly believe them. They are the perfect prescription for the ill-advised thoughts in our mind.

Failing Forward

FIGURE IT OUT

The second area that will help to overcome setbacks is the idea of "failing forward." In our attempts to achieve a certain objective, perfection is not the goal. Let me repeat that. Perfection is not the goal. To strive for perfection will be your Achilles heel.

So, if perfection is not our goal, and failure is not our goal, what then is the goal? It's best not to think of it as an end result, but rather what we gain in the process. It is all about who we become through our experiences. Anyone who is familiar with John Maxwell's work (he's an American author, speaker, and pastor who has written many bestselling books, mostly on leadership) might be familiar with the idea of failing forward.

The concept is based on the idea that you don't *just fail*. Failure is not an end result. It is a part of the learning curve, and as long as you still are moving forward, toward your goals, learning, pivoting, or adjusting along the way, then you're not failing! Every experience is a chance to learn something new—a way for you to reflect and evaluate.

(Spoiler Alert: This is actually one of the major parts of being resourceful—learning from failures by being flexible, being adaptable, and having commitment and perseverance to see your goals through. We'll touch base on these concepts in a few chapters. For now, it is important to know that you might not get it right on the first shot, or the second, or even perhaps the thirtieth. It might take many attempts, going back to the drawing board multiple times.)

Bill Gates once said, "Success is a lousy teacher. It seduces smart people into thinking they can't lose." So, start being grateful for all the lessons. Make peace with this idea so your expectations are set properly for success. In order to help you on your path, be prepared to learn through failures.

Taking Action

Lastly and probably most importantly is taking action—massive action. Even if you still have negative thoughts or you're telling yourself you won't succeed and that bad things will happen if you should attempt your all-too-crazy idea, and your mind seems only to think of the negative consequences, taking an action step and actually doing something is one incredible way to prove your mind wrong.

You've probably heard the saying that action crushes fear. It is amazingly spot-on. By taking a big, massive, in-your-face action step, you will soon lose all the fear that held you back in the first place. It is the fastest way to shut your brain up, because—here's the secret—taking action doesn't just eliminate those thoughts or push them aside for a little while; taking action eliminates your fear altogether!

Once you've done it, and your brain realizes you're still alive, that you didn't die, it begins to see that doing something you're uncomfortable with was merely a simple task. Your fear gets less and less authentic. You then start to gain some confidence, and your brain will quickly stop nagging you on how stupid of a decision it was. You then start to feel a bit silly, wondering what it was you were so afraid of in the first place.

So, just take action!

Because negativity will always play a role in your brain's space, it is critical that these three things become habits in your life. Thanks to the world around us, negativity will show up every day, if you choose for it to do so. Therefore, creating a habit of saying affirmations daily—in the shower, on your commute into work, or by making funny faces in the mirror while brushing your teeth—is essential.

The art of failing forward and continuing to take action steps toward your goals is the fundamental piece of growth. These activities need to become part of your everyday routine.

A great way to fail forward or to learn from your day is by reflecting on it. A simple journal entry at the end of each day is great for that. It will allow you to evaluate your patterns and identify how things went, analyze what went extremely well and what could have been better, and where your opportunities are in the days that lie ahead. Log those lessons so you can learn from the failures.

Another great way to help with failing forward is being grateful for all your crappy screw-ups. I once had an art teacher in college that used to call mistakes "happy little accidents." And it's so true! Life's lessons can surely be happy little accidents. That outlook was a great way to put a positive spin on a negative moment, because in the large scheme of things, it can be extremely hard to remember that one single moment doesn't shape your entire life.

It's a series of moments and a series of choices, over time, which shape your life. I know it can be hard to see that sometimes, especially when you're in the middle of something pretty crappy. Hindsight really is clearer. When you're through with the mess, I guarantee you'll look back and think to yourself that it wasn't that bad. You might even be grateful for it.

As bad as something was, there's always a silver lining, right? You might not even know or be able to see that it's a silver lining until years later, but when that moment hits you, when you realize you're able to pick up all the broken pieces and rebuild a new future, you feel pretty unstoppable. Use that as fuel to re-motivate yourself again.

Some other great ways to start practicing your newfound behavior is to volunteer for a new leadership role at your church or club, or to take on a new project at work or at home. There are so many little ways you can practice taking action without hesitation with a quick, "Yup, count me in!"

Think of the good things that will result. You'll learn new things about yourself, perhaps talents or skill sets you've never noticed. You'll get to meet new and interesting people outside your current sphere. Most likely, it will focus your attention on creating something good for others. Even better, perhaps by taking on a new project at work, you'll be in line for a promotion. If you volunteered with your church or organizational club, you could now have a huge impact on kids and youth development, influencing their lives in a positive way.

Lots of good can happen, if you aren't always focused on the negative (I don't have time; I don't want to be here on Saturdays; I already don't get paid enough to do my actual job, let alone more projects and work for the same pay; etc.). The list of negative thoughts and excuses will go on and on, but what you need to focus on are the positive ones (I can do this; I am worth it; I will achieve my dreams; etc.) and all the amazing things that will come when your mindset is positive and focused on what your life will look like in the future. Remember, your thoughts have very powerful effects on you, that determine what you do and who you are.

CHAPTER 1 IN A NUTSHELL...

- Everything begins with your thoughts—everything!
- Success isn't a skill set, it's a mindset.
- 3 ways to overcome negative thoughts are by using affirmations, failing forward, and taking massive action.
- It's a series of moments and choices that shape your life.

2

Habits

"Successful people aren't born that way. They become successful by establishing the habit of doing things unsuccessful people don't like to do."

—*WILLIAM MAKEPEACE THACKERAY*

Habits. That word always seemed to be a heavy one for me to use. Instead, I prefer to use words like "routine," or "practice." I'm even okay with the word "pattern." I think I prefer these words to "habits" because I've attended sports practices, I was forced to have a school routine (you know, where your parents force you out of bed every day, just in time to catch the bus), and looking for patterns seemed to be a fun game to solve.

The word "habit" has continuously felt toilsome, probably because I have attempted and re-attempted to build some habits that still aren't quite habits in my world yet.

I have fought many years to create good habits—normal ones like better eating habits (this is still tough because of my love for ice cream), waking up earlier (also tough, especially when you have a toddler), and working out regularly (this one's a challenge because I simply don't like working out anymore). I am saying all this so you realize I'm just like you. I've had the same thoughts and the same challenges you have when you focus on changing your habits.

When it seems like you finally get your routine established or you're making consistent progress, life happens to throw you out of whack. For example, say you decide to go on a health kick just before summer. You're all excited and making great progress daily, for several weeks. Then you go on your family-planned vacation. Just because it's a vacation, you think to yourself, *I can splurge! Just one day of eating French toast instead of eggs won't hurt. Yes, let's order dessert tonight—we're on vacation! No, I'm not going to work out today—I'm sleeping in so I can relax and enjoy my vacation.* Sound familiar? Whether you've actually said any of these words out loud or not, I know at some point you've probably thought them in order to justify your choices. Ever had a "cheat day" built into your diet plan? I thought so.

There can be many things that interrupt our momentum and what we are striving for. When you let yourself off the hook, you go back to your comfortable, normal routine. I have outlined some fantastic things you can do to build good habits, routines, practices—whichever word you want to use—and be successful at following them.

Start with Realistic Expectations

It's extremely important to start with realistic expectations. Otherwise, you're setting yourself up for failure. You can't implement too many new habits at one time.

You need to start with one and build other habits on top, once the first one becomes established. This is called habit stacking and is outlined in the book called *Atomic Habits* (add that one to your reading list). The tactic of stacking habits has proven well when looking to start some new ones. When your brain is hyper-focused on reconditioning your behaviors, that's when it's easier to add another one.

Habits are about the subtle, tiny things you do every day that lead to huge results in the end. If you haven't read the book called *The Compound Effect*, I highly recommend you pick that book up next. Darren Hardy lays out this idea so perfectly.

Losing 30 pounds doesn't happen overnight. It happens when you start exercising ten minutes a day, every day, and over the course of, say, eight months, you lose weight. It takes discipline, patience, and grit.

All great skill sets needed to become a more resourceful person should begin with setting realistic expectations—and we'll dive deeper into these in the next few chapters.

Be Sure the Right Systems Are in Place

Most people don't fail at creating their habits because they don't want to change their ways. Many do and are willing to go to big lengths to see they can improve. The problem that tends to hold them back is not in a lack of desire, but in the systems—or lack of a system—they are using. Quoted directly from James Clear, author of *Atomic Habits*, "You do not rise to the level of your goals. You fall to the level of your systems." The right systems have to be in place for you to follow and be able to continuously repeat them.

Stay Consistent

The biggest word to emphasize when focusing on habits is *consistency*. Whatever you do, do it daily!

FIGURE IT OUT

Whatever you want to change, fix, or improve, do it daily.

The thing with habits that makes it so challenging to create a new one or kick an old one to the curb is what we discussed in Chapter 1, your mindset. Your brain will tell you that's it's "more fun" to order pizza and drink a beer on Saturday while watching a college football lineup than it would be to hit the gym for an hour and come home and eat grilled chicken with brussels sprouts, or that just because it's the weekend, you should make pancakes instead of the boring egg whites you ate five days in a row already that week. Discipline is hard because your brain feels like doing something else; something that's fun.

Your brain will do everything in its power to convince you that you need to revert back to the way you've always been and to operate the same way you always have, which is the worst place for any of us to be—a place called "your comfort zone." This is the place where you feel safe, the place you feel confident, and the place you know and are all too familiar with. But the comfort zone is the last place on earth you'll want to be because you can't grow, learn, or be challenged if you're in it.

The comfort zone is where your self-doubts and limiting beliefs live. It's where your brain feels it's in control and will begin sabotaging you by keeping you from taking any risks, thinking any bigger, or believing that you can achieve your wildest dreams. The comfort zone is where you're at ease, and when you're at ease, you're not on fire. In order to trigger action, you must be struck with emotion—emotions like excitement, anger, passion, and even fear. All these are needed to catapult you into taking actions you wouldn't normally take. So, in order for you to feel compelled to take actions you wouldn't normally take, you must create the environment that will force those emotions to rise to the surface, creating the emotional surge required of you to take massive action toward your success. That can only be found outside your comfort zone and with the consistency of your daily routine, where you form the right habits.

I know that you are in the right mindset, you're focused on changing for the better, and that you aspire to be the very best version of yourself. Therefore, you know you have to step outside that box of being comfortable.

One simple way to get uncomfortable is to focus on one small habit. Let's use our exercising example again.

Say you want to lose 30 pounds, you're not a fan of gyms, you don't like free weights, and you really don't want to have to go out and purchase any new equipment like tennis rackets or soccer cleats. Since you have a pair of old Nikes in the closet, you decide to dust those bad boys off and just go for a run. Now, if you are not used to running daily or even at all, you might want to start with just walking around the block first, or perhaps just do a walk/jog interval (those are great cardio by the way).

The point I want to make is these are small, easily accomplishable goals—walk around the block, jog for ten minutes, do 25 crunches. You need to ease into your new habit. In this case, slow and steady will win the race, for sure! Remember, the key isn't performance. Your goal isn't to break world records; your goal is to remain consistent.

Here are a few tips for when you're creating a new habit that will help you to succeed at keeping it a habit:

1. Do it daily (yes, you're correct, you don't skip Saturdays or Sundays).

2. Do it at the same time each day.

3. Do it until it becomes as familiar as your toothbrush.

The first two are pretty self-explanatory so let me just jump right to that third one. It is my own little theory that I call "the toothbrush test."

I'm sure many of you brush your teeth twice a day, every day, without even telling yourself to do so. You'll never be on your commute to work wondering, *Did I brush my teeth this morning?* And for good reason! Brushing your teeth is a habit, one that you've formed since you were probably two years old, and it's the perfect model for all other habits you wish to form.

When I started my personal growth journey, habits and consistency were a huge struggle for me. Even more frustrating was that I couldn't figure out why. It was because I didn't have the right systems in place. I couldn't understand why I couldn't change my workout routine, why I couldn't get up at an earlier time in the morning, or why I couldn't say my affirmations daily. I would have really good days where I would achieve all the things I was looking to achieve, perhaps about 70% of the time. I told myself, *At least I accomplished that much, and I can re-commit tomorrow.*

The truth is, I set myself up to fail by going from zero cardio to attempting to run a 10K. Then told myself I would run that much every day. Do you think that worked out well? Heck, no! My expectations were not set properly, my lungs were not in shape enough, nor was it a system I could repeat. I certainly hadn't run a 10K consistently every day before that, so I needed to change by running a few days a week and then build up to seven days a week. I needed to start with ten-minute jogs that led to me being able to complete running a 10k race.

I learned this about twelve months after I had set that initial goal, when I accidentally stumbled upon an old journal. I picked up the half-written journal (another habit I wanted to do consistently that turned south after about two months). It was dated exactly twelve months earlier and it was like reading from the Groundhog Day's script. I was back at square one, re-committing to the same goals that I had failed at just a year prior. I had reverted back to my old ways. I had written all my new routines and goals I wanted to work toward, and as I read through it, I felt two polar opposite things. One, I was extremely motivated, and I learned that I was still excited and eager to achieve everything I wrote down twelve months ago. But secondly, and more disappointedly, I learned that I was still no further along than I was the year before.

I hadn't made any progress. I was the same person, doing the same things, still in my comfort zone, and getting the same results. It's no wonder my newfound, so-called "habits" were extremely short-lived. I couldn't possibly keep up with attempting to run ten kilometers, learning French, journaling, meal prepping (that one didn't even make it past a week), writing, reading, and setting new financial goals so I could afford to travel more.

I had set myself up to fail by trying to be 100% successful in all these areas.

The lesson learned from that was to just pick one, whenever starting a new habit. Only one, building it and building it until the system allows you to remain consistent. Then and only then can you move on to the next one you wish you accomplish.

What does all this have to do with a toothbrush? Hold on, I'm getting there.

It was that day I decided I was going to take one of my goals and do it until it became as familiar as my toothbrush. The toothbrush was the benchmark, when I knew I could add on another habit. And then another and then another, until all the things I wanted to incorporate became habits. I told myself, *If I can brush my teeth, I could start running daily. I could start journaling daily. And I could start writing daily.*

I know, I know, I know, you're probably thinking that brushing your teeth is like a two-minute task and to complete a workout is like an hour-and-half time commitment, which also requires a wardrobe change. Of course, it's easier to have brushing your teeth a habit, with working out being a constant struggle. This is where I encourage you to be resourceful!

This is your first test. If you had to figure out a way to find an additional 30 minutes in your already jam-packed schedule, could you do it? If you had to find an additional three hours, could you do it? I'm here to tell you if you can find 30 minutes, you can find three hours. We'll talk heavily about this in a later chapter on time-blocking and scheduling. The point I wanted to focus on now is that you'll know you've made something a habit when it becomes as familiar as your toothbrush. Do you only brush your teeth Monday through Friday and take the weekends off from focusing on those pearly whites? You sure don't! (At least, I hope you don't.) Do you ever wake up at 2 AM to go brush your teeth or randomly decide at 4 PM that it would be a good time to brush them then? No! The vast majority of people brush their teeth in the morning, when they are getting ready, and in the evening, before going to bed. So, the activity of brushing your teeth is at the same time every day.

One really neat thing is that up until now, your brain has been working against you, planting all those seeds of limiting beliefs and negative thoughts, telling you not to go for something you truly desire, and keeping you in your comfort zone. But here's where the magic starts to happen. After you've created a new habit, your brain will start to work

WITH you. This is the game-changing shift that occurs.

If you can master your mindset and create new, better habits, the rest is mostly like being in "cruise control mode," because your habit is now a normal part of your everyday life, without you having to focus heavily on it, or having to force yourself to do it. Remember, humans are creatures of habit. Your brain loves routines. You don't love having routines; your brain does. As you learned earlier, your brain thrives on knowing what is going to happen or what you are going to do because that keeps your brain in the driver's seat. It feels comfortable and likes knowing what to expect. It likes knowing you're safe and harm-free. So, now that you and your brain are both on the same page, by creating positive habits in your life, unlimited potential and abundant dreams are yours for the taking!

The key with this is that you will need to keep overcoming the power of the mind and always creating new and better habits and skills. So, you must prepare yourself that this will be your formula for every new undertaking you set out to achieve. You will have to get over these two hurdles, time and time again.

Start practicing with one new goal now. Take on one new habit at a time. Master that into your daily

FIGURE IT OUT

routine before adding on another habit. Otherwise, you will be setting yourself up for failure down the road.

You won't be successful if you're shooting for a 180-degree change. It's the tiny, one-degree corrections over a longer period of time that you're shooting for. Then, when you introduce another new habit, and you focus on making tiny, one-degree changes over an extended period of time, the results will be astonishing.

The concept of habit stacking is vital to your success. Build one habit at a time, slowly make your improvements, add more as you progress, and you will see a whole new person emerge—a person who is now disciplined enough to create the habits that will allow them to succeed.

CHAPTER 2 IN A NUTSHELL...

- Be realistic when setting new habits.
- Start small and focus on one-degree changes, because they will compound over time, and lead to a massive transformation.
- Stay consistent. NEVER miss two days in a row.

3

The Realm of Possibilities

"Your imagination is the preview to life's coming attractions."

—*ALBERT EINSTEIN*

How do you know what your possibilities are? Or what you're capable of?

That's sort of a trick question, in that you can't really answer it until you push yourself beyond your current capacity and further into more of what is possible for you. How do you do that? You first need to define yourself in terms of your possibilities. Self-awareness is a huge key that can help you understand yourself clearly.

What blocks people from reaching for their dreams and all that is possible isn't their lack of desire or their aspiration to achieve, but rather a lack of awareness in themselves. We are the first ones to put self-imposed limitations on our own dreams. If you want to understand why, re-read Chapter 1.

When you are aware of your limitations, you know how to begin to overcome them. The resourceful will challenge and question their potential, in hopes to maximize their lives to achieve all that could be possible for them. Remember, resourcefulness is a skill that everyone has. Most people aren't aware they have it and most people hardly ever use it. If more people could tap into that resourcefulness and harness it to think differently, it would arm them and allow them to bridge the gap between where they are currently and where they would like to eventually be.

What I want you to realize is that resourcefulness is teachable. It is a skill you already possess; you just don't use it. You need to teach yourself how to use it, through practice, just like when learning to play soccer or the violin. Once you learn it, I know it will dramatically change the way that you think, open you up to more opportunities, and enhance the decisions that will allow you to ultimately change the path of the life you're currently living. Here's where we dive into understanding more about harnessing the power of being resourceful by thinking! Remember, you are still in the foundational phase, which requires lots of thinking.

FIGURE IT OUT

First things first. You have to learn to think in what I call the realm of possibilities. What in the world does that mean? Let me explain. The realm of possibilities is the place where any and all things are possible. There are no negative vibes, doubts, judgments, obligations, or bad ideas. Sounds pretty great, right?

How do you get to this realm of possibilities? It involves less travel than you're probably thinking, for it's inside you now, in your mind. Stay with me, for a second—and think back to when you were a kid, or if you have kids now, I want you to think of how they act. To a child, what's possible for them? Practically anything, right?

I remember when my daughter just watched the movie FROZEN for the 164th time. She rambled off every line as she danced around the living room. Then she grabbed two throw blankets off the sofa. She wrapped one blanket around herself, draping it below like a wedding dress train. She handed the second blanket to me and wrapped it around my neck, like a shawl, to cover my shoulders. Then she declared, "I'm Elsa. You're Anna!" We exchanged a few lines and acted out a few scenes—quite impressively, I might add. She wanted to keep playing but I said she had to get cleaned up because her dad would be home any minute for dinner. She told me, "No dad! No dinner! I'm Elsa. You're

Anna." She continued to stay in character for a long while after that.

The point of this story is that she completely disappeared into a world AND believed it was all true; it was her current reality. To me, it is amazing that she can be in the living room playing Connect Four one moment, then throw on a blanket and she's a princess the next! Why, as adults, do we not live that way anymore? Some would argue we have to grow up, yet why does being an adult mean we have to be responsible and just pay the bills and be boring? Because we have to? Because we don't have a choice, if we want a great car or nice house, we have to be a slave to a boss? If we want our kids to be able to go to college without taking on student loan debt, we need to work tons of overtime? Or even to provide simpler things, like paying for dance shoes and recitals? The point is no one should be living their lives that way—out of obligation and because they have to.

You should be living your life as if anything is possible, regardless of your current circumstances. What you desire *can* be yours, and you can pursue that possibility without judgment and without guilt.

In the realm of possibilities, you can only think in terms of how great things will be and how different life will look. That's not to say that it won't be hard to get there, or that you won't have to make small sacrifices first—believe me, both of those things will be true, but the end result will be so much better. At the risk of sounding super lame and cheesy, you can do anything you want to do, and become any person you choose to be. What's even better is that it's not up to other people. That decision of who you are and what you want doesn't rely on others judgments or opinions. It only relies on your ability to believe and continue to think that your life can be exactly as you desire.

Now, I want you to pretend, like you're a kid again. What do I mean by that? I mean I want you to put yourself in a three-year-old's brain. Kids, when they are little (ages two through five), don't have an understanding of the world yet—as we know it, at least. This is an important lesson for us adults to learn. In the realm of possibilities, EVERYTHING is possible for children. As adults, we go into despair, as though all our dreams will never happen.

Resourceful people, however, in the realm of possibilities, react similarly to children. They think big. This is great for two reasons. One, they don't get discouraged and lower their ability to fight against those limiting beliefs that will creep back in. Two, if they act on their idea, chances are that it will have a major impact. Remember, you want to change your life! If you're unhappy with how you've led your life up until now, or you're feeling somewhat stuck in a rut, so to speak, then you need to let go of all those self-imposed thoughts that keep holding you back. Forget being "normal," forget what you're "supposed to" do, forget being "reasonable." Your life isn't about any of those things. It's about chance, love, adventure, and overcoming struggles, so give yourself the permission to aim high, and let yourself dream in the world of possibilities.

When you're able to let yourself think in the realm of possibilities, it's important to be as specific as you can. Think of it like this: when you walk into a restaurant, you don't just order by saying, "I'll have some food, please." Instead, you're very specific. You pick exactly what you want from the menu. You specify the Italian sub on whole wheat bread with no mayo. If your meal were to come out wrong, you would send it back to the kitchen to fix it, right? Perhaps then you'd order something completely different that would satisfy you and your taste buds. If you were to be so detailed and explicit with something as little as a sandwich order, there is no reason you can't apply the same standard to your life. In fact, it's more important that you *do*, when it comes to your life versus your lunch order!

But that's what people do. Most people will go through life saying things like, "I just want to be happy," and then they wonder why they are always unhappy. Here's a clue, wanting to be happy isn't specific enough. The universe doesn't know how to help you become happy because it doesn't know what happiness is to you. You have to be specific, to the tiniest detail of what happiness is for you. If you're one of those people who doesn't have a clue what happiness looks like, then you need to be clearer on what it means. What does an extraordinary, happy, fulfilled, rewarding, accomplished life look like to you? What does it feel like, every day, to be living an extraordinary, happy, fulfilled life? If that is too deep for you, start with a simple question. What's keeping you from having the life you desire right now? Then use your response to begin eliminating those things from your life. These and other questions are important to ask so you can uncover exactly what's holding you back. You can then begin your journey of becoming resourceful to then being skilled enough to go out and achieve all that you desire from this life. The clearer and more vividly you visualize a goal, the easier it will become to acquire it.

Remember the saying, "Don't ask why, ask why not?" That's thinking in the realm of possibilities. Thinking this way will help you with your current tasks at hand while also helping you learn to become more creative, to think outside the box, and to approach a problem from a unique angle. These are all the things resourceful people do and they serve them well on their path to success.

Also, getting out of "the ordinary" is fun. Others will most likely notice a new, vibrant way about you. Energy is contagious and if you bring the same level of excitement to your new work project as a three-year-old does about going to Disney, everyone's bound to notice.

Lots of people can be indirectly affected by your behavior. There are tons of opportunities that you will create. They may not provide the exact results you were looking for, but sometimes that can be okay. The universe tends to know what it's doing in that regard. It can lead to an even bigger or better result for you; one that you never thought possible to begin with. When those days or moments happen, be sure and celebrate them in a big way.

Another extremely important reason why thinking in the realm of possibilities is so critical—especially in today's world—is because of the lack of contentment that is out there. *The Business Journal* conducted a poll of the workforce and discovered 80% of people said they were unhappy and would like to quit their current jobs. Eighty percent! Of that 80%, less than 1/3 of those actually quit and moved on to something else. So, the majority of people out there today currently feel unsatisfied, unfulfilled, and hate their jobs, yet still work there. What kind of life is that? It could also be the negative self-doubts and other people's influence that leads to you staying paralyzed in your current job. If you're that person, the one who feels unfulfilled and currently unhappy with your work, you must be resourceful to find another solution, and I'm here to help with that.

There are so many ways to make it happen; you just have to find one that works for you and your situation.

Money = freedom. If you have money, you have options and choices in life. That's why most who don't have a lot of money feel stuck. The word "stuck" is intentional, because if you don't have money, you don't have choices. Therefore, you are stuck or forced to continue as your life is because it keeps a roof over your head and food in your belly. This is where thinking in the realm of possibilities will help you see other options that are available to you.

I promise you, if you are disciplined long enough to correct your finances, your world will start to look a lot different—whether it's renting out a spare room on Airbnb, selling some old stuff online, or taking an extra side job to start accumulating some extra dough. I know all that sounds exhausting but remember, it's all temporary. A year or two will fly by, guaranteed, and you'll be set to start making some different choices.

You may declare that you want to take on a side gig or take action on the photography business you want to start. You feel excited and ready to take on the world. Then, a few weeks or months later, you are probably back to your norm. I'm sure many of you can relate—any New Year's resolution is a perfect example of this. Every year, on January 1st, people make all sorts of declarations that this will be the year they lose weight, this will be the year they are debt-free, this will be the year they move or start a new job, or whatever the case may be, yet by February, 90% of those resolutions are broken—after just a few short weeks! This has to do with a number of things like a lack of commitment, no accountability, unrealistic goals, etc. Yet one important factor to note is the motivation, because all motivation is short-term fuel. The level of motivation you bring to your dream of quitting your job or losing weight will die. Achieving goals don't require motivation, they require you to have discipline. That's why the right habits are important to create. Otherwise, you won't be proving anything to anybody. After the excitement and motivation wears off, all you are left with is the painful longing of hope and what could have been. Perhaps, next time, it'll be different—when you've reached the point where you don't ever feel like working out any more or you don't even care if you don't like your job, you're at the point where you are okay with letting yourself off the hook and the only thing that might keep you going is to prove all those naysayers wrong. It's no longer for you or about your desire to achieve it; it's about all those people who didn't believe you could—those who told you that you would fail and all those who said it wouldn't work.

What's attractive about working from home is the pleasure of not commuting or doing a job you don't feel is rewarding, where you're not making a significant impact. The majority of people today need to feel they are impacting something, in some way. If you don't feel that level of fulfillment in your job, it will be the cause of all the negativity in your life. It will build and overflow into other areas of your life—your health, your self-worth, your relationships, your finances, and your spirituality. All these areas of your life will also suffer the same unfulfillment.

Let me paint you a picture. If you're stressed at work or miserable at your current job, you might come home feeling *blah*, so you grab a beer to help take the edge off. You're too exhausted to cook dinner, so you order pizza. You're mentally drained, so you turn on the TV so you can relax. Each day repeats itself in a gloomy, sad routine, and your weeks all begin to look the same. Meanwhile, your self-worth is at rock bottom because you don't feel proud or confident in your work or habits. Your health will be short-lived because you're relying on beer and takeout (not high in nutritional value), without any exercise routine built in because you're too tired. Your finances will probably be tough, because you're spending too much money on takeout or the convenience of grab-and-go food, and your Netflix or cable subscription. Your relationships with your loved ones aren't top priorities because you don't want to have negative conversations with people when they ask about your day or talk about the problems you're facing. You want to be left alone to relax. The kids are doing their homework, your spouse is doing their own thing or perhaps is off to work themselves, so there isn't much quality time spent growing the relationships stronger. Spiritually, you feel that there isn't much good in this world or that it's all out of your reach for you, so your faith is lowered. Beliefs that you once held slip further and further away. It is so easy to have one little area of your life affect the quality of many other areas. That's why it is important for you to focus on doing something that you love, that brings you joy!

On the top of a blank page, write down this question: What does my life look like when I'm happiest? Then write your answers. Think in the realm of possibilities.

Now, notice that I didn't ask what your goals are or what you were looking to have or achieve in your life. I simply asked in the realm of all that is possible. What does happiness look like for you? Do you have three vacation homes? Are you debt-free, are you running your own business, are you learning a second language? Are you driving a new car, are you working on or in your dream career, are you writing big checks to your favorite charity? Are you singing backup for Justin Timberlake, opening a school library, inventing a new, earth-friendly eco-fuel? Who are you with? Who are the people you see or interact with daily?

You can literally write down anything. Nothing holds you back when you think in the realm of possibilities—not people, not money, not technology. ANYTHING and EVERYTHING is a possibility.

Take ten or fifteen minutes to write how you desire to be living your life. This will shed a tremendous light on what your goals are.

Once that activity is done, take the big, "someday" vision of how you want your life to be and scale it back to today, listing ideas for action steps and goals needed in order to make it all happen.

This will show you what you cherish and what's important to you. It will help reveal to you what makes you happy and what makes your heart sing. Remember, when something is passionate enough, you need not know how to make it all happen, you just need to anchor to the why you desire it.

I promise you that if you're in tune and know your *why*, the *how* will just show up—like magic! The universe has tons of gifts and if you're not open to receiving them, you never will be able to receive them. You must remain open to possibilities. If you think in the realm of possibilities, you will experience a life of unlimited possibilities.

CHAPTER 3 IN A NUTSHELL...

- Don't limit your potential by limiting your thinking.
- Be extremely specific and have a clear picture of what it is you desire.
- It's okay to be a kid again and dream big, with a world of possibilities.

FIGURE IT OUT

Part 2: BEING—Building the Skill Sets of the Resourceful

This next section is all about *being*—who you are being, what you are becoming, and all the experiences you have had that created the being you are. The word "being" has such a unique definition in that it has no definition at all, just a series of other synonyms—words like existence, living, reality, vital force, entity—all describing the very nature or essence of a person. When explained like that, it's no wonder that when we use it in a sentence, it becomes extremely powerful.

When we say we're being careful or being productive, we mean we are currently living in that state of whatever we say we are being. It is our actual reality at that moment. You've probably heard this in many ways or another, but one of Jim Rohn's most popular quotes states, "Success is not to be pursued; it is to be attracted by the person you become." If you have been exposed to or studied Jim or anyone like him, you will know this is true.

Success shows up when you become the person capable of achieving success. There's a lot that goes into becoming successful. It's not just about hard work, stubborn grit, or the yearning to achieve. A lot of people aim to be successful, and yet the truth is that very few people achieve their desired outcomes. I believe that's because it comes down to your level of resourcefulness, because in order to "become" implies that you go on a journey, you experience, you learn, and you grow.

The only way you make it to the other side, the side in which you arrive at success, is by having the ability to be resourceful. So, in the next few chapters, we will dive deep into this idea of "being," by identifying all the skill sets that resourcefulness poses.

4

Problem Solving—Being a Problem-Solver

"Most people spend more time and energy going around problems, then in trying to solve them."

—*HENRY FORD*

If you read the introduction (hopefully you didn't just skip it and start at Chapter 1), you will remember that I gave the exact definition of what it means to be resourceful. It is having the ability to find quick and clever ways to overcome difficulties. More simply put, it is about problem-solving.

This is why problem-solving is the first skill set you need to learn in order to become more resourceful.

I'm sure that you have had your share of life experiences, including many personal or job-related experiences where you've needed to really think out a solution to something.

A fun example of this, and what's all the rage right now, is the notion of escape rooms. If anyone out there hasn't yet been to or tried an escape room, they are super fun! Each room has its own theme, with a mission or task that has to be completed before your time is up, which is usually about an hour. You can also pick your level of difficulty, so if you decide to go for your child's birthday party, you'll be able to adjust the level for the kids. If you're up for a super challenge, or really competitive work parties, you can go with the highest level. To escape from the room, at whichever level you choose, you have to be an active problem-solver.

A lot of movies and books have great plots and storylines like this, too—James Bond, Batman, or Disney cartoons, like puppies Bingo and Rolly, who go on a new adventure every day to solve problems. Many books and movies have characters who are faced with extreme challenges like saving the world, battling their arch nemesis or just helping the little squirrel find its big squirrel family.

The need for problem solving is all around us, in our everyday lives. Some days, they might be tiny little problems. Other times, they could be more serious. Have you ever gone somewhere and discovered that you left your purse or wallet at home but need to grab gas on your way to work? I've been there! Have you ever left your laptop at home when you need to present a speech at school or pitch an idea at work? I've been there, too! This probably sounds familiar to a lot of you because we are faced with problems every day. Some problems are more extreme than others. Hopefully, those don't occur in your life very often. For the most part, we face slight problems that our brains go on a mission to solve.

Problem solving is a great skill to have. You might be wondering how one *learns* such a skill. Is it truly something that can be taught? Rest assured, it can.

Some ideas will naturally pop into your head that you could start to take action on, to bring you to a solution to the problem. Chances are, the first few ideas may not work. So, how many ideas do you go through before you give up? This is the question I have for you because you can only become a problem solver by actually *solving the problem*—not by coming up with six ideas that won't work. That's just called brainstorming.

Your goal as a problem solver is to reach the solution and actually solve the problem! If you shift your thinking to an idea that will form a solution, more solution-based ideas will come to you. Each might be slightly more ridiculous than the first one but—trust me—you're making progress toward your solution.

How do you begin problem solving? Well, how do you learn to do anything else? If you wanted to be better at basketball, you'd practice more. If you wanted to get better at golf, you'd practice a few extra rounds. If you wanted to get better at dancing, you'd practice, maybe by signing up for dance lessons. So, if you want to get better at becoming a problem solver, all you need is practice.

The simplest way to learn is through the art of repetition. I'm sure you have experienced some type of problem to solve. Have you ever double-booked an appointment time? Or needed to be at Pee Wee football in the east end of town and then soccer practice an hour later in the west side of town? Have you ever been driving to work and gotten a flat tire? Basically, anytime you've ever had a plan, and the plan didn't go the way you thought it would, you were faced with a challenge (problem) and you needed to figure out a new plan (solution).

There are two ways to approach problem solving. One is with time and the other is with no time. These are all challenges we need to solve. More often than not, we have time to plan or prepare to solve them. We get enough lead time from our boss on a project to complete, we know our children's schedules a month ahead, or we are so good at problem solving already that we can predict a situation is about to occur. Then there are other times that we must simply think on our toes and act fast! Ever had to throw a speech together quickly, prepare an agenda to a meeting you didn't know you were supposed to be attending, or make the game-winning shot? If you've experienced any of these or other somewhat similar situations, you have conditioned your brain to learn to problem solve. These are great experiences to have.

To most people, solution-based thinking comes easy. For those of you that really struggle with thinking quickly on your feet, or aren't sure where to begin because it's frustrating and stressful under pressure to think at all, here are a few steps that will help you learn to become a better problem solver:

1. **Assess the situation.** Usually, a problem will start with a response of "Oh, crap" or "Oh, no!" or "I forgot my..." or "How in the world are we going to make it?" The important thing to do first is understand the real problem at hand and know what the desired outcome should be.

2. **Know your lifelines—no one succeeds alone!** This is a huge lesson for everyone out there. If you ask anyone who has experienced success at a high level, they will tell you that it didn't happen without the help of others. They didn't get there alone. You need to think of who you could call, ask, or seek advice from. Perhaps that

person knows some information that would help you or has a tool that you could use. It can be a friend, a co-worker, a stranger in a gas station, or even Google. Get out your phone and ask Siri or Google for some information! The world today is not short on information or facts; it's short on people lacking the desire to take action steps. But not you! You're learning to problem solve so you can be one hell of a resourceful and successful person.

3. **Use tools.** You've probably seen someone use a credit card or paperclip to unlock a door, right? Some people with long hair have used a pencil or pen in the absence of having a hair tie handy. Ask yourself what tools you have at your disposal to try and use. If you've ever seen a lady with a giant purse, chances are she has everything from a sewing kit to a spare pair of socks in there! That's just how many women roll—we use something once and then we never take it out of our bag, just in case the need will arise again. A lot of guys carry Swiss army knives because those things are useful for anything! What other tools are at your disposal?

4. **Practice by playing games and solving puzzles.** This is fun and it works! Play

FIGURE IT OUT

Sudoku—that game will get your head to think like you've never thought before. First, you know it's a solvable game. Second, there are specific strategies that work from time to time. Other times, you have to switch it up, finding a unique way to get all the numbers in the right rows and columns correctly. If you possess an ounce of competitiveness, you'll achieve this in record time. There are many brain apps out there now to help your brain stay stimulated, so download a few and use them. You can also play board games or other games. Chess, Clue, Connect Four, and Battleship are all fun ways for you to learn to problem solve while having a few laughs and even spending quality time with people.

Problem solving opportunities are everywhere. You just have to view them as such—as opportunities for you to practice getting better and more resourceful every day.

CHAPTER 4 IN A NUTSHELL...

- Solutions are all around you—keep looking!
- Know your lifelines—no one succeeds alone! Who can you reach out to?
- Practice will help you improve your skills.

5

Learning and Curiosity—Being Learning-Based

"Formal education will make you a living; self-education will make you a fortune."

—*JIM ROHN*

What would happen if you stopped learning?

What would your life look like if you didn't discover new things?

The ability to learn new topics, new information, new procedures, or new systems is critical when it comes to being resourceful. It's important that we never stop learning. Resourceful people love to learn!

If you don't currently love to learn, it's possible to create the inkling to do so. You can begin by reading a new book or signing up to take a class. You could go to your local community college, city library, or Apple retail store to obtain information for some type of class, whether it's a "Spanish for Beginners" course, learning great public speaking skills at your local Toastmasters event, or just a way to learn how to sketch, draw, and paint with your iPad. The opportunities to learn are out there! As you become more resourceful every day, you'll start to take notice of opportunities all around you that allow you to continue to learn.

Another great way to learn, if you're short on time, is by using YouTube. If you watch a "how to" video, you'll learn some pretty cool stuff.

Growing up, I never learned the essential, little things. Sure, I took a Home-Ec class, but let's be honest, everyone knows those are cakewalks; an easy way to get an A. In 2004, I already had "senioritis," so there was no going back, no matter what class I signed up for. However, later on in my life, I wish I had paid closer attention, so I could at least know how to sew a button on a shirt or a pair of pants. There are many times where that would have come in handy. So, for all you other kids who breezed through their senior year, I recommend YouTube because it taught me how to sew a button on!

Education is all around us. There is no reason why you can't load your toolbox with more knowledge, information, or skills. I promise you, down the road, it will most certainly pay off.

FIGURE IT OUT

Each moment to learn something new will allow you to expand your thinking and allow you to become more resourceful! When you're resourceful, you're on the road to achieving any goal you set out to achieve.

I'm sure you'll agree that the world evolves way too fast for you to keep up with it. In this day and age, it's critical to be learning, evolving, and open to change. Plus, trying something new can be incredibly fun.

If you're hesitant or if it's not in your nature to be up for something new, set a monthly or quarterly goal to come up with a new idea or activity, and then do it with a group of friends. There are tons of art workshops around most towns nowadays, and anyone can gather two or three friends, a bottle of wine, and go make some beautiful art projects with a block of wood and some paint. Perhaps you can approach your boss and/or manager at work and inform them that you think it's time to get more training, or that you want to learn more about a different department. Ask them what programs are available through your company. They will most likely reward your initiative.

Another great resource for education and learning opportunities is Eventbrite, an event management and ticketing website. Many people who are hosting seminars and training events will post the event on

Eventbrite. Simply go to the website and type in your city's name. All sorts of topics will pop up in your area—some even for FREE! Another incredible resource is TED Talks. There are so many videos that will help you in any area you wish to improve, on topics you find interesting, and on topics that you simply know nothing about. You should make a habit to watch a TED Talk video at least once a week or on a monthly basis.

Learning New Skills

Most of the time, if we hear the word "skills," it's in reference to hard skills, such as a talent, where you physically take action—like being able to sew a button on, carpentry skills like fixing a fence or building furniture, or even a creative skill like photography. Then you have another type of skills, called "trait skills," which are skills such as leadership, integrity, decisiveness, and adaptability. These are the traits you can't physically see but notice in people all the time. These are the skills I'm referring to in this section.

Trait skills are learned and enhanced, when you practice them over and over.

How do you practice a behavioral trait skill? How do you become a better leader, or learn how to become more decisive? It's no surprise that these skills are also enhanced through repetition and practice.

These traits are learned through the practice of your experiences, and all your experiences, added up together, are what determines your level of any particular skill. So, now I have to ask, how are you growing and practicing them? In what areas of your life are you outside your comfort zone?

Once you have a desire to grow these traits, you will need to put yourself in a position and be ready to use them… but how? You are surrounded by groups of people, problems, and situations every day, so look for opportunities in your life to lead your families (for example, organize a huge family reunion trip with 34 cousins), church groups (for example, sign up to run a mentor or support group or become involved with one), or volunteer to coach your kids soccer team (you'll be surprised how well other children will listen to you, even if your own don't). I know it sounds simple—that's because it is. Any of these experiences will help you to develop the type of skills needed to become more resourceful and become a person capable of achieving great things.

When you're consistently learning, you're consistently growing. In the world of personal development and self-mastery, this is important! You might be thinking, *Yeah, but I'm the person that's struggling, I've been working so hard and can't seem to get ahead.* If you're that person who is struggling with your life (asking questions like "Why me?" or saying things like "My life is crap. Nothing everything goes my way!"), then I suggest you get out of your own head, change your environment, and challenge your current way of thinking by learning something new. What's the worst that could happen? I'll give you a hint, the answer is NOTHING! You have nothing to lose, you're already feeling like you've hit rock bottom, and by going to a class or getting yourself to learn something new, you'll find wonderful, new people to hang out with. You'll learn something new about yourself—perhaps a great talent you didn't even know you possessed. You'll be exposed to different environments. Seeing other people achieve things (especially things that epitomize what your idea of impossible is) becomes infectious. The result is that you've just told your brain anything is possible and you can do it, too!

In my experience, this is what I think tends to scare people the most. It's not that they are afraid to take action; they are afraid of what comes after the action, or what they discover in the process. They then feel a sense of obligation for that continued life pursuit, and they use that as the excuse for never starting.

FIGURE IT OUT

For example, I hear people all the time who claim they don't know what they are passionate about, or that they are struggling to find what their passion is. I believe that's a lie they are telling themselves. The truth is that it's an excuse, and if they knew their passion, they would be accountable or expected to be on a life pursuit to enjoy that passion. However, in our world, we think that's not okay to do, because we have responsibilities. We have to go to school, then get jobs, have insurance, and provide for our families. We have been conditioned by society to think this way, to stay within the realm of what's expected of us, and to do just that—be mediocre, make a living, and retire semi-happy—when the truth is that you have a raging passion for fly fishing, photography, baking, or something else and you'd much rather spend your time focused on one of those passions. But the world has convinced us that to start a photography or other type of business would be a huge challenge. So, many of us have bought into this type of thinking, that we can't open a bake shop, and that there's no possible way to make money from fly fishing, so these passions are just hobbies you get to enjoy every once in a while.

I'm here to free you of that disbelief!

There are probably tons of ways to make money from whatever it is that you're passionate about, but the fear sinks in, not in discovering what you're passionate about, but rather that you'd have to find a way to make money at it. That's where fear sits, when you have to prove to the world it can be done, and the deck is stacked against you. That's where people get held back. This is where those limiting beliefs tell you to just stick to your accounting job, commute to a boring office, and wait it out, until you can take your retirement package because it keeps you safe and that's what people expect of you.

These are excuses and I won't stand for that! Life is meant to be an adventure and your life mission should be to enjoy every bit of that adventure—the ups, the downs, the wins, and the struggles. Enjoy the entire journey! I challenge you in this because it's critical to a life well lived. Don't make the excuses that you don't know what you're passionate about. Don't live a life of regrets. Take a chance and please, I beg of you, don't deprive us of getting to know the world's greatest fly fisher!

Use your ability to learn, grow, and discover your resourcefulness to use your passion as a way to achieve your income goals and provide for your family. You owe it to yourself to enjoy what you do. When you do that, you'll be providing an amazing example for your children to see that it is possible to create your own desired path so they don't have to overcome the same hurdles you did. You will be programming their brains by showcasing them a way to learn and to grow. More importantly, you'll allow for those experiences to shape the trait skills they need for them to become the successful bakeshop owner, fly fisher, or the most sought-after photographer in the business.

Be the Curious One

Because learning is two-fold, the second part of learning is to always stay curious. Personal development, educating yourself, and discovering and improving your skills are just the beginning. The follow-up step is being in a state of curiosity. This is another weapon that resourceful people use and use well.

On your journey to becoming more resourceful, you will want to remain curious. Start evoking that inquisitive nerve in your brain to ask a few questions. Start inquiring about things or events that you normally aren't interested in. You'll be amazed at how quickly you will start enjoying this newfound way of learning and growing in curiosity. Start somewhere simple. Kids are great at this! They are constantly asking, "What's that?" If you ever need a good example of curiosity or a way to learn through curiosity, just mimic a four-year-old.

Those that continue to learn and those that stay in curiosity are those who will be well armed in the field of resourcefulness! If you're not there yet, start little by little, each day. When you're learning how to become more resourceful, you're consistently pushing yourself, and you're consistently challenging yourself. Therein lies the beauty. You're not staying still. Instead, you're in a motion of consistent progression. You're learning a lot about yourself. You're investing in yourself and who better to bet on than you?

We are all capable and possess huge potential. When you're being resourceful, you're standing up for YOUR potential. You're sharpening your sword, every day! I guarantee that if you continue to do that, it will lead to the powerful results that you seek.

CHAPTER 5 IN A NUTSHELL...

- NEVER stop learning!
- Read books, watch TED Talks, take a class, and use Eventbrite.
- Meet new people because they can introduce you to things faster than you can discover them.
- Stay curious. Wonder and ask questions.

6

Adaptability—Being Adaptive

"We have to be stubborn about the vision, but flexible about the journey."

—*JEFF BEZOS*

Step 1: Identify the solution. Step 2: Execute the solution plan.

Have you ever heard of a plan where hope or optimism was used as the strategy for how something was approached? Or a plan that was executed using the first idea or thought that came to mind? Most likely not. An original plan was probably followed up with Steps 3-20, all detailing what to do when Step 1 failed, forcing you to go back to the drawing board and create new solutions or change the approach. Rarely does something ever work out perfectly the first time, which is why the third skill of resourcefulness is adaptability.

Being adaptable requires you to be able to quickly match or coincide with whatever you're surrounded by. Whatever the circumstance or situation, you need to be able to quickly switch gears and adapt to the new conditions at hand. It sounds pretty simple, except we, yet again, find some big challenges with this because we are not prone to change easily.

In fact, most adults struggle with change and accepting it, especially older adults. We've all known grandparents that just are who they are, who won't change for anything. They've lived their entire lives a certain way, and it's a bit harder for them to accept that change is good or even necessary. They've been doing what they have been for so long, and maybe they just don't want to admit that changing—or some changes—can be good.

Perhaps you're in the same boat, where you've consistently ingrained certain actions into habits, or ideas into certainty. Whether in your personal or professional life, I guarantee you have some routines. We all become set in our ways. Remember when we discussed your mindset and discovered that the brain loves routines? It loves knowing what to expect.

Being adaptable will force you to challenge your mind and convince yourself to trek into the world of the unknown.

FIGURE IT OUT

Some people say they don't mind change; that they love and embrace changes. I hear people say this all the time, yet quite often they are more resistant to change than they think. I would almost bet a million dollars that what they are claiming is not true, on all accounts.

For example, I am around a lot of people on any given day, and the majority of those people say they are flexible, that they're not picky, and that their ways are not set in stone, but when the time comes for them to exhibit their "go with the flow," laid-back approach, it doesn't show up, especially when they need to implement a new system at work or adjust a daily routine. They just rant and rave about how silly it is to them, or why they need to be doing it at all. That's when you know if they are truly adaptable. Sure, it's easy to say you don't mind change when things, people or circumstances change for the better. That's not an adjustment most people are upset with. It's when the changes are daunting, stressful, tough, sad, disappointing, or difficult—those are the situations that make it hard to adapt to. This is where resourceful people truly shine. They thrive on turning a negative situation into a positive one.

Be cautious of the people that say, "But that's not how we use to do it," or "We've always done this way," or "That's how it's always been." These are people who will not be open-minded about new ideas, improvements, or changes. They are the people who will challenge you in a negative way.

Depending on the change, it might take some time to adjust, but once you're on board, don't hesitate. It's better to embrace the change than put yourself in an emotional state of turmoil. Usually, change requires actions to be different, systems to be different, or people to be different.

Resourceful ones know that change really is a good thing, because it is usually an improvement or for the betterment of something, including the action process toward a goal or achievement. They know that changes will benefit everyone down the road and it might take some time for everyone else to catch up. That's okay; they need to get moving onto the new goal. The new purpose is there, change happens for a reason, and resourceful people know the importance of embracing good changes.

However, in some cases, you might not be able to see a change coming. These are the times you might need to adapt and embrace it rather quickly, which will require that you use other resources available to you. So, it's important to know the environment you're surrounded by and what options you have. It's also good to have a back-up plan and to know, if worse came to worse, where you could go from there. Whether it's a project at work, a vacation you're trying to navigate, a personal problem or situation you're dealing with, or whatever the case may be, resourceful people always remain adaptable.

Being in the Girl Scouts was a great way to prepare me for staying adaptable because their motto is "Always be Prepared." That is true for an eight-year-old girl selling cookies and it is true in almost every situation I have encountered throughout my adult life.

Be prepared to switch gears, if necessary—no questions asked, no thoughts to ponder. Be ready to react and to adjust, as the situation requires you to. If action must be taken, resourceful people simply adapt.

Adaptability and Life

Adaptability will take time to develop, so you need to be patient with yourself and your growth curve.

Many folks on a journey to become more resourceful struggle *big time* here, because it can be extremely difficult to focus on a new way of operating your life. However, just remember to focus on the good that is coming from the changes. Keep your perspective focused on that and I promise your brain won't fight you and resist the change. You will learn to embrace it! You will start to welcome changes. What you used to find stressful, you will now approach with a sense of excitement and exhilaration.

I'm sure you don't need me to tell you that life will throw its fair share of curveballs at you. Sometimes, the best parts of life are the unexpected ones, and it's in adjusting and adapting to a new norm or way of life that you're going to have to get used to.

One interesting thing with adaptability is that it's your ability to change but it's also your willingness to *be* changed. That tiny word changes a lot in that sentence and it is a critical word for understanding what that means. Not only is our world changing and we need to learn to adjust to it, but we—and the roles we fulfill (such as being moms, dads, wives, husbands, siblings, mentors, friends, etc.)—all change, too.

Our experiences shape us and allow us to become better at who we are, but if we are unwilling to adapt, grow, and experience changes, how can we learn? It's important to remember to use the art of adaptability on your road to becoming more resourceful.

You see, it's not a matter of "Can you be adaptable or quickly jump on board and get behind a new idea or initiative?" It's more of an "Are you the type of person who is capable of doing so?" If you're not—yet—you need to become a person who is, because nothing in this world stays the same and nothing is concrete or guaranteed.

Being adaptable isn't only required for you to be more resourceful; it's required in order to enjoy living your life.

Adaptability Starts with Being Open-Minded

Adaptability requires that you be open-minded. You have to be open to changes that might take place. Do most people like change? Heck, no! Most people fear change, resist change, and complain about change. In order to become more resourceful, you will need to understand the importance of maintaining an open mindset.

The idea of pivoting or being able to pivot from one skill to another is a great asset to have. Simply being able to change direction on a project mid-stream, or being open-minded enough to see other possibilities or ways of achieving your goals is critical in helping you get a lot further along and closer to that goal—seeing that the old way isn't always the most efficient or effective way, understanding that you may need to switch gears, at any moment, trying another approach.

I'm sharing these different phrases in hopes that you're relating to them in some capacity, having used or said them, at some point, in your own life, that your work experiences or travel adventures have required you to take an alternate route or change direction at some point.

It's important to take a moment and examine all of your options.

Usually, when unexpected changes occur, you are required to act quickly, but I also want to encourage you that if you have some time on your side, thoroughly think through each option and then select the best one.

New changes can be really good. They force you to be aware and to pay attention. I think we could all use that reminder, at times! Adapting to change also helps you achieve high levels of resourcefulness!

CHAPTER 6 IN A NUTSHELL...

- Remain open-minded—always!
- Be flexible with your journey.
- Adjust your sails, every once in a while.
- Always be prepared—apply the Girl Scout's motto to your life.

7

Observance—Being Observant

"The most dangerous person is the one who listens, thinks, and observes."

—*BRUCE LEE*

You might be wondering how one can learn to be observant. Well, I'm here to change your world, remember?

In order to be more resourceful, you must learn to start being more observant. Paying close attention to detail is great when it helps you gain information, which is what resourceful people do with the details. They tuck them away for future use, or to gain further insights about something.

Resourceful people understand that information is all around us and you can learn it just by watching what's happening.

Have you heard of the fictional character, Sherlock Holmes? He's a perfect example of someone who uses the power of observation. Another good one is Jason Bourne; he's a key observer of every situation. Now, I know these two examples are not real people, they are characters in TV shows and movies, but I wanted an exaggerated example to make the point of what a person who is highly observant would look like. Hopefully, it worked.

You're probably nodding your head, to acknowledge the point was made, but thinking to yourself, *I'm not a trained CIA agent, nor a master detective with a British accent.* That's okay! You just need to be able to mimic them and their trained eye, in your everyday life, and more importantly, be able to understand and use the information you learn by observation.

Below are a few fun ways to help you get started.

1. People Watch

We will start with my personal favorite, people watching. You can learn a lot about people, society, relationships, social cues, norms, and many other things simply by watching them. With over 7 billion people on this planet, you're not short of opportunities to watch people.

The next time you're at the airport, the park, riding on the subway to work, in line at your favorite restaurant or coffee shop, at a mall, or stuck in a traffic jam on the freeway, put down your distracting texting device and start noticing the people, not in like a creepy, stalker-ish way, but just in a normal "I see you and I'm learning from you" kind of way.

2. Behavior Profiles

You are probably familiar with some sort of personality profile or perhaps have read some articles or books on human personality behaviors.

The DISC personality assessment, the strengthsfinder assessment, and the Myers-Briggs Personality Type Indicator are all types of behavior profile tests and help to tremendously understand the way humans behave. This is an important piece to really understand. That way, when you are watching people, you can identify with people's traits as you watch their behaviors. Some will have some pretty strong, telltale signs of who they are, depending on the situation you're observing them in.

There are also some great YouTube videos that give examples of such behavior profiles. Be sure to watch some different examples when getting in an elevator or driving in a car. Next time you're in a car with some friends, take note of the personality of the driver, and the next time you're on your way up to the 35th floor of a hotel, notice the other people's behavior profiles around you.

3. Body Language

People can say a heck of a lot without using words. When observing people, be sure to also study their body language. There are great articles on Pinterest these days and books on Amazon that can teach you all about body language.

There's an entire psychology behind little things like one's posture, facial expressions, the pace at which one walks, how one holds or positions their hands, and where their eyes glance to when answering a question. All of these and many others are huge signs of one's attitude, if they are interested or disinterested in a conversation, if they are being truthful or lying, and if they are confident or nervous.

Body language plays an important part in our lives, such as how shifting in your chair could be the death of you on an interview, how certain looks or glances could be too inviting and send the wrong message, and even something so nonchalant as a head nod could mean the difference between success or failure when trying to close on a huge sales deal.

Did you know that over 90% of our communication is actually non-verbal? That's right, it's 93%, to be exact.

Of that 93%, 55% is classified as body language and the other 38% is tone of voice. Therefore, people essentially are telling you more or saying more without actually using their words. So, the more you know and can learn about body language the more you'll be able to notice someone's demeanor, and quickly pick up cues about their emotional radar.

4. Listening

Believe it or not, listening is a great way to observe. Listening *actively* is a great way to learn from those who are speaking. When people speak, their word choice and the tonality in their delivery is important to take notice of. Word choice can tell you a lot about the person or the situation as well as how a person feels in response to the conversation.

Here are some tips for really good active listening:

1. Let the other person speak and don't interrupt them.

2. Listen with the intent to understand, not with the intent to reply.

3. Be sure and look at the person speaking; stay present and in the moment.

4. Look for the non-verbal cues (body language).

5. Use empathy.

6. Focus on the overall message, not just the words.

7. Be careful not to jump to conclusions or assumptions that you know what they are trying to say. Pay attention to what they aren't saying, too!

5. Art Classes

Sign up to take a drawing or painting class. This will force you to pay more close attention to things, such as the immense detail of colors, placement, lines, or the music playing in the background. In a studio class, you will get totally focused on the object in front of you, and with that object being the only thing you must focus on, you will begin to see tons of new details you've probably never noticed before, even if it's something you've seen many times before, like an apple or a bowl of fruit. You will begin to notice many new interesting things about the fruit, the bowl the fruits are sitting in, the table that the bowl is on, etc. It will cause you to have a new eye or a fresh perspective on something that you wouldn't normally pay attention to. Try it out!

6. Evaluations & Reflection

Use evaluations. Ask a friend or a co-worker to rate you on a scale of 1 to 5, or print off a few questions from an online assessment (you'll find tons if you just google "evaluation" or "assessment"). People will show up differently when they know they are going to be evaluated or will be receiving feedback from peers. I know this from personal experience. It was terrifying at first, but I sure learned and improved in the end.

It happened in a class I took on how to be a good trainer/presenter. I teach a lot of classes and trainings, so I thought that I might as well learn how to level up my skills and stay sharp. The only catch was that you're in a room full of peers, all with an evaluation form that gets filled out, and you're evaluated on things that you did well and feedback is given for areas where there is an opportunity for improvement. Then, once you finish giving your presentation, you just stand there, in front of the entire room (with your own thoughts and critics running through your head). Your peers then point out and verbally tell you (while you're standing there) what you did well and where you can improve. It's really intimidating. I would literally apply deodorant before it was my turn to present!

I've actually taken that class a few times (I even signed up for the advanced level one) and I could feel myself improving on my facilitation skills tremendously! There was a noticeable improvement in my level of preparing as well as how much time I spent going over the material before I taught it. There was an improvement in my speaking skill and a huge improvement in my use of crazy hand gestures. There was also an improvement in my ability to relate to the class and how to help them absorb and learn the information. There was an improvement in a ton of ways!

Now, your first step doesn't have to be signing up for a training class or a public speaking engagement (although your local Toastmasters meeting would be an amazing place to start if you did want to start enhancing your presentation skills). You could start with people you know and ask something as simple as, "What do you think about my level of communication?" You could mention leadership, adaptability, time management, or all of them—whatever it is that you want them to provide feedback on. Ask, "How well do you think I communicate? Where could I improve, to become a better communicator?" Ask these questions, and then have an open mind when hearing what they have to say, even if it's not what you want to hear. Take their constructive criticism for what it is and use it to improve.

All of these are some great ways to start you off in becoming a better observer. Once you dive in, you'll find that being observant will help you become more resourceful! You might see a solution you wouldn't have normally seen before, simply by training your brain to quickly pick up and notice tiny details that can reveal important information. You're training your brain to look around and to take notice of behaviors, things, people, body movements, and word selection… which will allow you to have an edge or appear more intelligent, when really you're just being observant.

Something else that works well, is using the art of reflection. Without reflection there is no change. So do a check- in at the end of the day. Stop to journal about an experience or event that took place. Explore what you learned, where you succeeded and where there might still be areas of opportunity for growth.

What you will find (in addition to being resourceful) is that you will be present or more "in the moment." You'll truly start to appreciate the beauty in the world around you. There is beauty on the subway, there is beauty while standing in lines, and beauty in people watching—whether you're at the airport, park, or mall. Being observant will open your eyes and help you to take in the experience of that moment, of the smells that fill the air, the music playing in the background, the sound of a child's laugh, the comfort of a familiar voice, the heartbreak of a couple, or wise words from a caring mother. You will begin to see the world in a very different, unique, and beautiful way. So, start being more observant!

CHAPTER 7 IN A NUTSHELL...

- Pay attention - there is information all around you
- Get off your phones, get off of autopilot, and take notice of the world happening around you!
- Participate!
- Be present in the moment.

8

Creativity—Being Creative

"Creativity is intelligence having fun."

—*ALBERT EINSTEIN*

The last skill set of resourcefulness but certainly not the least, is the skill of learning how to be creative. When you're being resourceful, it's important that you also learn to harness your mind's ability to be creative and allow your brain to think creatively.

What do I mean by all that? Many people in today's society would think that you either have creativity or you don't—that you are either an artist or a person that has no artistic ability at all; that you are either "the creative type," unique, and different, or are not creative but a run-of-the-mill, methodically straightforward shooter. You might be seen as left-brained or right-brained. You get the idea, right?

In the business world, we see creativity differently. We will use this business example in the way you think about the word "creativity."

Outside of business, people tend to think that creativity is the link to artist ability, and that could have been where your mind went, too. I'm not referring to artist ability here, so for the purpose of this chapter, we will focus on the business use of the word "creativity."

In the business sense, creativity is more about one's ability to think by using one's imagination. Perhaps another good word that might help is to use the word "originality." It's the way you think and how you think that's linked to your level of creativity. Something original is usually deemed to be creative or clever.

For example, the invention of the light bulb—a concept once thought by society as an impossibility—is credited to Thomas Edison because he possessed the ability to be creative. In his creativity, he discovered 10,001 ways to build his idea and to bring his idea to life. His first 10,000 ideas failed; his last one gave us the incandescent electric light bulb.

From Edison's experiences, it's important to know that you need to become an idea machine on your path to learning to be more creative, or to surround yourself with people who are idea machines. The more you work on exercising your creative thinking, and the more you challenge yourself to generate new ideas and concepts, the more you will grow in the field of creativity.

It's important to get these brain juices flowing! Once they start, the ideas usually get better and better. I'm sure you've been in a situation where you've felt this firsthand or watched that momentum show up in people as the ideas just flow from one person to another. An initial idea begins to build and build and before you know it, everyone's excited and ready to put actions in place! This is creativity forming. Even if you never end up using any of the ideas, you are conditioning your mind to think bigger, to think differently. You're pushing yourself and others to ask questions such as:

- What else?
- What's another way?
- How can we get the results we are looking for?
- What do you need to do differently?
- Wouldn't it be fun if…?

Therefore, instead of defaulting to what the majority of others do and wallowing in defeat, or even worse, coming up with excuses, you are pushing your brain to continue going a million miles a minute, searching for a solution to the problem, or searching for a new approach, where you can begin to see a solution as a possibility. When creativity shows up, you have a lot of options to move forward with.

How does one achieve this? How does one develop and measure creativity? To view creativity in action, one has to bring those unique and original ideas from the mind (from the intellectual world) and put them into action (into the physical world). Try this, either at your next staff meeting, sales meeting, or board meeting. During your morning pow-wows or afternoon huddles, gather your team together for an exercise. Have your business partners and co-workers do a brainstorming session of ideas. Put a theme in place for that week, or a problem the organization is faced with, and just brainstorm for some new ideas. If you're stuck and perplexed about a decision, turn it over to the people around you. Put on some music, bring in coffee and/or snacks, and create an environment that is free from distractions, which will allow you all to bounce ideas off each other.

Thinking outside the box will create an open, playful space of excitement, adventure, and possibilities, all which can really help the team to formulate a solution, idea, or theory. It may get you out of a sticky situation or you might have a new go-to approach to solve a problem.

FIGURE IT OUT

You know that old saying, "Two brains are better than one"? That's exactly what I am talking about. I truly believe people have great ideas and are capable of sharing constructive thoughts. Keep in mind that most people will only share when they are asked to (you have to prompt them) and feel that they are in a safe environment to express their ideas. So, make sure those two things are in place. Otherwise, you may not get much participation.

Having resourcefulness can be fun, and creativity is a way to demonstrate that fun! It's one of those things that work well when you don't put too much structure or too many guidelines around it, so be sure to avoid rules when asking others to participate. Also, don't judge or discourage any ideas. You can poke holes and criticize the ideas later, if need be.

Avoid saying all the reasons why an idea won't work and just focus on getting all the ideas out, on the table. Some of the most terrible ideas end up being the best ones. So, even if it feels a little silly or crazy to implement and try one, if it involves a low risk, you might want to try it, anyway. Sometimes, it is okay and almost necessary to be a little adventurous and see what happens. You might pleasantly surprise yourself by having fun and being creative.

CHAPTER 8 IN A NUTSHELL...

- Have FUN!
- Think outside the box.
- Brainstorm and mastermind often, so you can become an idea machine.
- Surround yourself with people who challenge you to think creatively.
- Foster a safe environment for others to generate and share ideas.
- Don't be afraid to be adventurous and try something new.

9

Productivity—Being Productive

"Productivity isn't about being a workhorse, keeping busy or burning the midnight oil. It's more about priorities, planning, and fiercely protecting your time."

—*MARGARITA TARTAKOVSKY*

Productivity is a tricky thing to experience. In the coaching world, it is one of the top things that I hear people desire most. To improve their productivity and master the art of time blocking. A lot of times, we think that if we can just keep ourselves busy, we are being productive and accomplishing what we need to accomplish, yet that couldn't be farther from the truth. In order to be insanely productive and achieve the big results you desire, you need to learn the skill of time-blocking.

The skill of time-blocking is important to talk about because it seems to be a common denominator and one that successful people have figured out. I wouldn't really include it as being a part of resourcefulness *per se*, but it is a skill that will help you a lot on your personal development journey, so that you can achieve success at a high level. Here's what I know about time-blocking: tons of people struggle with it and successful people have mastered it. This skill hits people hard because we can easily be distracted by practically anything. We are currently living with the world's worst distraction of all time: our smartphones. We are consistently scrolling through social media, checking emails, and taking photos of food.

Time is one of the greatest resources, and an extremely valuable one at that. I value time over anything else, as do most other people. How I get to spend my time, what I get to do with my time, and who I'm spending time with are all hugely important to me. At the end of the day, it's all about how we use the time we have.

We sometimes feel like there isn't enough of it, and that we need more of it. I am sure you have heard someone say, "There are just not enough hours in the day!" It's true. Time is a precious gift that we need not take for granted even though it is, in fact, one of the easiest things to be taken for granted, because it goes on, whether we use it or not. If it goes to waste, we'll just go to bed and a new day will start, but that shouldn't be our approach. For many of us who are looking to achieve success, it's important that we are in control of our time. We should not be focused on everybody else's idea of how they think our time should be spent, but rather focus on what's important to us and how we choose to use or spend our time. This is my goal for you because when you are controlling your time, how you want to spend it, and who you are spending it with, you will truly see the benefits of success and joy. You will truly achieve great things. So, it's important that you don't waste your time. One way to help you focus and use time as a resource is by managing it.

Time-blocking isn't just an idea of how to structure your day, or something you use just for the sake of your calendar looking pretty with different colors. Time-blocking is a proven productivity method. It involves you completing big and small tasks *one at a time* so you can get things done faster, be less overwhelmed, and more successful.

Before we get into it, let's say you're an accountant and your goal is to start your own business. YAY! Your own accounting firm! You will still need to work inside of your typical 9-5 hours, as you begin to grow your new business. So, you set a goal to make that happen, and you start becoming busier. You are now spending all your spare time brainstorming and preparing to start your business (you know, all the easy stuff first). Eventually, you'll need to start covering some living expenses or save up some money, so you can in the near future quit your current job to allow you to focus on your new business! That may consist of you spending a lot of time outside of your typical 9-5, doing things like driving for Uber, waiting tables at a local restaurant, picking up additional work projects on the weekends, or doing some other side hustle, just to get ahead. This is where people get exhausted because in reality, you'd rather be home enjoying time with family because the kids are off to bed at 8 PM and you want to see and spend time with them, too. Or you also have to go to the gym, because you want to stay in good shape—your health is important, too— but meanwhile, you get a text that says "Please pick up butter on your way home," so now you're running errands around town. It's madness. How is it possible to accomplish all the things you want to accomplish? This is tough when you now have added the role of entrepreneur to your existing roles and responsibilities of being a mom, dad, co-worker, husband, wife, friend, and pet owner—the list goes on and on.

I'm sure we've all felt as though there simply isn't enough time. We can't possibly fit it all in; we're humans who are spread way too thin. This is a lie that we have been conditioned to believe. I'm here to tell you there is enough time and that perhaps you're just not using it properly.

You're not being efficient and you're not dedicating certain tasks to be done at certain predetermined times throughout the day. A great quote I heard from Darren Hardy is, "You can do anything once you stop trying to do everything." That is an incredibly powerful and accurate statement. You can't be focused if you're pulled in 20 different directions. You're doing the worst thing that anyone could possibly do, which is to believe you are doing it all. Now, you can absolutely change your whole life, but you can't change it overnight, or by being focused on a million different things.

If you're focused on changing too many things or completing too many tasks, you will only end up stressed out, overwhelmed, unmotivated, disempowered, and unhappy. Raise your hand if you've ever felt that way. Of course, you have! That's not the goal for you; that's going backwards to the beginning (see Chapter 2 on habits). So, it's imperative to make a priority list of important tasks and what needs to be completed first.

There are many ideas of thought around productivity and using time effectively. In fact, there are entire books dedicated to this topic. The book called *The One Thing* is an amazing resource and contains tons of tools to help you stay on top of what's most important and what will help you achieve extraordinary results. Time-blocking is almost like a financial budget. When you have a budget, you're telling your money in advance where you want it to go. Time-blocking is just like that. You're basically telling your time in advance how it will be spent and pre-selecting what activities you will be doing during such time. How you use your time is critical to your success.

Time is a precious gift and it can aid you in your journey if you allow yourself to maximize it.

How to Maximize the Gift of Time

Time in the Car

If you have a long commute to work, you can effectively use your driving time to accomplish other things. You can listen to podcasts that align with your goals, to keep you focused. For example, if you're looking to learn about investing in real estate, want to learn another language, or want to learn how to be a better spouse or parent, you'll find a number of podcasts on topics like that.

Maybe you have important phone calls you need to make and a hands-free system in your vehicle to make them. Instead of waiting to call those people when you first get to the office, you knock them all out on the drive in.

FIGURE IT OUT

Waking Up Earlier

It's important to know all the little ways you can jump-start your day on a successful note. A big one is waking up earlier. If you struggle with hitting the snooze button or if you like to sleep in, be sure and read *The Miracle Morning* by Hal Elrod. You will learn a whole new, profound approach to your mornings and what you can accomplish before 7 AM.

Meal Prep | Lay Out Clothes | Technology

Plan out your meals for the week! Pack your lunch before you go to bed. Select the outfit that you will wear to work, the night before. Take advantage of technology and the services that are available. Order all your groceries online and have them delivered, so you're not running around trying to make it to the store. Buy an iRobot Roomba® (if you don't have one already) so the house gets vacuumed when you're asleep or at work. There are numerous different things you can do in advance that will help you. Try a few of them out and find your rhythm for efficiency so you can focus on what's most important!

Audit Your Time

There are many other great examples of finding extra time in your day and one of my favorites is auditing your day. I'm sure if you took the time to audit your day in 15-minute increments, you'd be amazed at how much extra time you can find. Those minutes really add up!

The problem is, we live in such a fast-paced, on-the-go, got-to-go kind of world that we feel a sense of accomplishment if we are moving fast. However, it's essential to know what you achieved in that amount of time. If you are not achieving anything, who cares how fast or slow you do it?

Time is not about going fast. In our society, we've been conditioned to think that it is a good thing to be going fast, or that multitasking is a great talent to have, and that we need to be consistently moving or be on the move because "time is money." Don't buy into that; that idea is wrong. It's more critical to know what you're doing during your time blocks and how you're using your time. For example, if your top priority is not what you are actually focused on during a huge part of your day, you won't be making any progress toward achieving your goals. You need to make sure that you have time to focus on that top priority and eliminate any

FIGURE IT OUT

and all other distractions until that top priority is completed.

Have you ever wondered how some people achieve everything they need to and aren't stressed going about their day, while others seem to be so overwhelmed, running around, only achieving some of what they need? What's the difference? How can one person do it and others can't?

We all have the same 24 hours in a single day and the same seven days in a week.

Why do the results differ so dramatically?

It comes down to time-blocking, to making use of the time available, and doing it in the most resourceful way. The key is being purposefully and strategically time-blocked.

Let me share with you a little exercise that might help. Ideally, we are supposed to sleep for eight hours a night. Most adults also work 40-hours a week, which equates to another eight hours a day. The average commute time in the United States, according to the U.S. Census Bureau, is 25.4 minutes, one way. That's almost one hour a day of travel time. Add those three things up for a total of 17 hours. Now, if you subtract 17 from 24, you are left with an additional seven hours in a day. That's an additional 49 hours a week and an additional 210 hours a month.

Here is what I recommend you do. Create a list of tasks you need to complete. They could be simple things, such as running errands, picking up the kids from sports practice, cooking dinner, going to the gym, working on a side hustle, planning your week, paying bills, calling your parents—whatever the case may be. Then write down how long each task will take you to complete—15 minutes, three hours, 40 minutes, etc. Then time block that into the extra 7 hours you have for that day. Note your day in 15-minute increments, because 15 minutes is small enough to waste but substantial enough to matter. It's like putting a puzzle together, where your tasks are the pieces, and they need to go in a certain spot (or time of day) in order to make the whole picture turn out right.

Another really good exercise to try is auditing how you currently spend your time. Take out a journal and write down all the things you did today, noting how long it took you to do each one. Do this for one week and you will be amazed at how much time is wasted throughout the day.

It's so easy to think we're being purposeful and using time productively when, in reality, we're not even close.

FIGURE IT OUT

The phrase "I don't have the time, or enough time" is the biggest excuse on the planet. If you feel like you don't have enough time, then you simply aren't using your time to your advantage. I'm not saying you can't spend time relaxing or enjoying things you love, or being with the people you care about.

It's important to get a little R&R in, too. Self-care is essential; know how much of it you need to recharge to be at your 100% for those in your life. So, don't mishear me; be sure and go to the movies, sleep in, and take time for yourself. Just make sure you've accomplished your top priority first, then enjoy all the downtime you want.

One of the many benefits of time-blocking is that you'll start to feel less stressed throughout your day. I'm sure you've had those days that you just knew would be a doozy, and to your surprise, the entire day went on without a hitch, flowing perfectly from meeting to meeting or task to task, hitting all your to-dos and deadlines. I call those days "the perfect storm," where it can be crazy busy, but all in a good and productive way. You will start to have more and more days like that if you learn to time-block.

Another satisfying thing that comes with time-blocking is having control. You will soon begin to feel like you truly are in control of your day, versus your day controlling you all the time. You will be less stressed, more productive, and be able to use your time doing what you'd like to be doing versus being forced to spend time on things you'd prefer not to be doing. That's the power of time-blocking. It puts you in control of your day, allowing you to make more choices that coincide with the version of life you want to be living.

CHAPTER 9 IN A NUTSHELL...

- Prioritize your most important thing!
- Stick to a schedule.
- Audit your time. How much are you wasting?
- Resourceful people fiercely protect their time—stay on course!
- Eliminate distractions from your environment.

Part 3: IMPLEMENTING—Taking MASSIVE Action

Implementation is the process of putting a decision or plan into effect. This is where you will take all the things you learned, along with all the skills you've built, and you execute them in a big way to achieve the results you aspire to accomplish. This is where you have to apply Parts 1 and 2 of this book to catapult you into where you desire to be.

Have you ever noticed a toddler that is learning a new skill for the first time, like how to walk, hold a fork, put on shoes, or get themselves dressed? Just think of one of these or any other example in your head. After the child's first attempt, what's their reaction? They fuss, they cry, and they whine, because they never master the skill on their first try.

All these skills need time to develop. Just to go to one of your friend's Instagram feed. I'm sure it's loaded with videos of their kids taking their first steps. They stand for a minute and take a step or two, then—boom—down they go. It takes weeks for babies to learn to walk, many meals for them to learn how to hold and use a fork the right way (not just wave it around in the air), and months or even years to get them to dress themselves properly. To this day, my toddler still struggles to put her own socks and shoes on, and if she does, they are almost always on the wrong feet.

This pattern continues on in life. As adults, we don't leave these traits behind us. Certain tasks are hard for us to do for the first time. Yet, what's our reaction? If we are good at it, we're surprisingly impressed with ourselves and chalk it up to beginner's luck. If we're terrible at it, we whine and complain and say it is something's or someone's fault that we didn't succeed. Regardless of the result, we don't continue to pursue the activity. We don't continue to incorporate a routine to improve or continue to learn. If anything, we might just revisit the activity once or twice more, but most likely not. We tried it and it didn't stick, because implementing anything new takes time.

As adults, we can get just as impatient and frustrated as a baby learning to walk for the first time. Yet, with enough attempts and despite the many fall downs, over time, the baby starts walking one day. The big difference is that adults don't continue the pursuit. We don't see the result we seek right away, so then we rob ourselves of our potential. If we just gave ourselves a bit more time, we'd probably develop and grow into who we are meant to be. So, it's important that you are always implementing, or always are in "action mode." Taking action is the only way you will crush the fears, eliminate the doubts, and have enough attempts to get good at something.

This section is designed to help you through all the implementation parts, where the messy stuff happens—the parts where you get frustrated and impatient. When you're in "action mode" (implementing), it's going to bring you a whole new level of awareness. It's going to expose you to yourself. It's going to feel terrible. Yet, it's critically important you keep implementing, because as long as you're in "application mode," taking action, you will become a better version of yourself. So, get ready to implement!

10

Ask Powerful Questions

"I never learn anything talking. I only learn things when I ask questions."

—LOU HOLTZ

To interrogate your reality means that you question everything—in a good way, not in a bad or "I'm second-guessing everything" kind of way, but by productively questioning and probing your train of thought.

I'm a big fan of questions. Most resourceful and successful people ask really good, thought-provoking questions—of others *and* themselves. The reason questions are so powerful is because they put your brain in "thinking mode," and when you're asking them, they keep you in control.

Questions can serve you well, no matter what role you're operating in. For example, as a coach, asking questions is critical to my clients' success. In my job/leadership role, questions help bring clarity to my tasks and projects. And whenever I'm in a training class as a learner, I always ask myself questions. *Am I the best student in the room? What's my level of engagement? Am I taking good notes? Am I fully participating, asking questions for clarification? Am I putting action items on my calendar?* (Pro tip: don't just write down what you want to do; save yourself the repetition and just book that note or the key takeaways right into your calendar. You learned another good tip in the time-blocking section of this book, to pre-fill out activity times on your calendar, so just book that note into a time slot. Depending on what the note is, I like to put notes in the *thinking/brainstorming time* I have blocked out in my calendar, or if it was researching something, I'd book that in my *planning time block*. That way, I'm embedding the note in my head by writing it AND I'm committing to a day and time in which that idea will be worked on!) So, by asking a few simple questions, my brain goes into "thinking mode" and I focus on how I can be the best student in the room. See, asking questions works great for any role you are currently in.

FIGURE IT OUT

At this point, you have the five basic skill sets down that resourceful people have acquired, plus the bonus skill of time-blocking. You can take your resourcefulness to a whole new level by asking powerful questions.

Remember, resourceful people need more information; they crave it with their inquisitiveness. They seek knowledge and they stay curious, and one easy way to get information quickly is to simply ask a question, because anytime a question is asked, someone answers it! If the answer is a "No," or "I haven't a clue," that's still an answer.

Answers generally provide lots of information to you. Let's say you ask a co-worker a question and they give you a response of, "I haven't got a clue." What did you just learn? We could conclude a number of things. Perhaps this is their first week on the job and they don't know which way is up. Perhaps they work in a different department and you just happened to catch them as they were strolling back down the hall from using the restroom. We most definitely learned that if in the future we have similar questions related to this topic or field, to *not* ask them, but to find someone else to consult instead. See, even with that crummy response to our question, we still could learn a lot of information, if we stopped to think about it. We'd learn a heck of a lot more if we asked more questions of that same person, digging a bit deeper into what they did or what their position was, how long they've worked there, or if they knew someone else that might have the answer.

Asking questions is a huge part of what makes resourceful people successful, because they gain information. It's great to ask questions of others but in this chapter, I want you to focus on asking questions of yourself. The only way to discover what it is that you truly desire is by asking some questions. The only way to help you uncover a game plan or roadmap to make it all come to fruition is by asking yourself some questions. The only way to know, understand, and evaluate where you are in the process is through questions.

Questions will continue to play a big role in your personal development journey.

Sometimes, we think we are going through life one way (or we seem to tell ourselves that) and it isn't what other people see or is our actual reality, because our vantage point is biased toward us. It's completely skewed, from where we stand. Therefore, the only way to get out of your own way is to ask yourself some really tough questions. Think of it as a checkpoint. You are simply doing a check in on where you think you are and where you actually are, and can make any adjustments, if the two don't match.

FIGURE IT OUT

Asking questions is a great way to reflect. It's been said that you can't know where you're going if you don't know where you are. That is so true! If you don't have a starting point, how will you map out the plan to the destination?

It's critical to know where you are in this moment of your life right now, which habits and skills you have at your disposal, and which habits and skills you still need to develop. The second most important thing to know is where you want to end up. What is the goal, the dream, or the vision you desire to achieve? This is a simple two-question assessment.

Identifying where you are right now and where you desire to be is just the beginning, but the problem most people have is that they are focused on all the messy stuff in the middle. Resourceful people do not put that at the forefront of their actions. They acknowledge that the unknown is well yet unknown. They stay focused on the present. They are aware that pitfalls will arise, but they know they will deal with them, when they do. They ask questions to evaluate their current situation. *I am here, so what's my first move? How do I get from here to there?* They also know that they make progress one moment at a time.

First, you must clearly identify what it is that you desire—to start a baking blog, to open a yoga studio, to focus on being a better parent or spouse? To get your finances in order, get out of debt, and start building wealth? To put your health first and eat cleaner?

Whatever the case may be, Step 1 is you have to have a clear understanding of what it is that you desire.

Second, have a clear understanding of the measurement. Otherwise, how will you know if you are making any progress? Let's use the first example of a baking blog. You know you want to start one, but will it be successful if you just register a domain name? Of course not. You need to set a goal that you can measure, like committing yourself to writing a post once a day for six weeks to build your content, or committing yourself to finding 1000 people who will subscribe to your blog in the next four weeks. You must be able to measure and track your progress. That's Step 2.

Growth and progress won't be a perfectly drawn line with a ruler, seamlessly going from Step 1 to Step 24. Growth is messy! It is one heck of a traffic-jammed, congested mess. It is a good thing it's what you want, even though it might be a challenge. Many of us love to accept a challenge. Challenges will keep you on your toes, sharpening your resourceful sword. Overcoming obstacles is what makes you the person you are. More eloquently stated, your challenges are what introduce you to your potential. For you only obtain knowledge and skills through experiences in life.

Remember what we talked about earlier? Resourceful people are great at solving problems, learning, being observant, accumulating information, and thinking creatively. We already know success comes from overcoming struggles. Tom Hanks said it perfectly in the movie called *A League of Their Own*, "The hard is what makes it great." Becoming resourceful is the key to success because you are more likely to get through all the hard struggles if you have a high level of resourcefulness.

Questions are your key to understanding. In this crazy whirlwind of a process, you need all the understanding and clarity you can get. Get in the habit and practice asking really good, powerful questions every day.

CHAPTER 10 IN A NUTSHELL...

- Get in the habit of asking powerful, thought-provoking questions.
- Questions are your key to understanding and gaining more information.
- Know who to ask for what you need.
- Have a list of questions to ask yourself, so you can reflect and measure your progress.

11

"No Dead End" Mentality

"There is no failure except in no longer trying."

—ELBERT HUBBARD

Understanding the skills and what it takes to become resourceful and having the desire to achieve your life's biggest dreams is fantastic. The entire concept of achieving success all starts by learning to become more resourceful, and hopefully, these chapters are helping you to see all the areas in your life that you can now practice becoming a more resourceful person. As you make progress, developing a "no dead end" mentality will help you on your journey to success.

We've all experienced many moments in our lives that weren't necessarily all cupcakes and rainbows. It's important to remind you that you have to keep your mindset positive and focused, because there will be times when you will encounter and come head to head with life's challenges and big struggles. Success is a journey. It's about developing and becoming. It's about the tiny 1% changes that we are focused on every day. It's easy to write a few feel-good, happy, motivational quotes, but when the time comes to overcome big challenges, will you be ready? I'm sure you would like to believe that yes, yes you will, thinking, *No problem, I've got this! I'll just handle life's shit as it comes at me!* That sounds great in theory, and the concept is simple, but by no means will it be easy for you to tackle or achieve when you need to start taking action. Throughout the years, I've experienced that many times, that notion of *Don't quit. Keep pushing. You only lose if you quit. If you just keep playing the game, the game is not over.* (As a kid, I used to do that, when playing cards. If you have ever played Rummy 500, and you lose 465 to someone else's 515, your suggestion is to keep playing to 1000, because if the game just continues, there's still a chance you can win.) Or if you challenge a friend in a game best out of 3 and they beat you 2 out 3, what's your first reaction? That's right, you immediately suggest, best out of 5! You see, by extending the finish line, you remain in the race.

Over the years, I've come up with my own theory for handling things because it's the only way for my

FIGURE IT OUT

brain to comprehend the notion of never giving up. I'm a visual person, so it's really the only way that I can envision not giving up in a physical sense. Even though we're all working toward different goals, my pursuits are different from yours, and my breaking point is different from yours, too. I will still share this idea and trust that it will help you to connect the dots.

My theory is that—for the resourceful ones and those in pursuit of being more resourceful—the road you're on never leads to a dead end. There is always a Plan B, a Plan C, or even a Plan T. You'll have to go through a lot of terrible ideas or silly thoughts to find the best way to approach your problems, situations, or life circumstances. That is merely a fact, and what leads to the transition from being resourceful to becoming successful is that you never ever hit a dead end. You don't quit; there isn't an end goal.

You will always and forever be on the pursuit of something bigger and better, increasing your standards, increasing your dreams, and increasing the people you surround yourself with that align more with where you want to go. So, use this analogy of never hitting a dead end when you feel trapped, when you feel as though there isn't anywhere for you to go, and when you feel that there is nowhere for you to turn. Even though you might feel those ways, that doesn't mean you're without options. It's important that you don't misinterpret a roadblock for a dead end. When you have your experiences (either good or bad) and when you hit those roadblocks, don't ever, ever let them become a dead end. Change your mindset and adopt a "no dead end" mentality. It's just my way of saying don't quit, don't give up.

Keep calm and find an alternate route. It's interesting to me that most people give up when they are near or close to the finish line. After all the stuff they have endured, this is when they can finally see the light at the end of the tunnel—the finish line to their initial goal—and yet, they still give up. Ironically, I thought it would have been the opposite—that they would have given up after the first few attempts. *Forget this, I'm out. This is not for me, thanks. I'm moving on, to start something else.*

We make some progress and then make a little bit more progress, and because we have so much momentum and excitement, it is a bit easier to overcome those first few hurdles. Then we get worn down, we get tired, and we lose sight of why we even started in the first place. It's in those moments that our motivation dies, and we begin to second-guess everything we've worked so hard for.

You may be thinking, *Yes, I've experienced that! What's wrong with me?* Nothing! You're human.

FIGURE IT OUT

Setbacks happen. Sometimes, life just sucks. However, we all experience the right things at the right times, and roadblocks are a part of the journey to self-development—to growing, to learning, and to developing. They are a part of it because nothing worth having comes easy. John Maxwell said, "Everything worthwhile is uphill." Everything! This is why only a few will achieve the success that they desire. Many fall short when they see a roadblock because they turn into a dead end. That is their breaking point. Only a few continue on, with steadfast perseverance, which is why it's important for you to add this "no dead end" mentality to your resourcefulness toolkit.

Remember, this is what the resourceful do. It may take you a few attempts to get through it, but when you do, you've become the person who has grit, determination, and perseverance, who now knows you are capable of achieving great things.

On Sunday mornings, one of my friends and I usually have a girl's brunch. We catch up on what's happening at work and in our personal lives, talk about the latest news, and discuss the latest struggles that we encountered. We usually meet at Bonefish Grill, which has an all-you-can-drink mimosa menu on Sundays. You can get one giant breakfast plate and endless bubbles for $20. So, needless to say, it's our go-to spot on Sundays.

One particular Sunday, we spoke mainly about our obstacles and the recent challenges we were having in our lives. Because we had no good news to share, we had a few extra mimosas that day!

However, toward the end of our conversation, as we were walking out to the parking lot, to wrap up one of her thoughts, my friend told me she had heard a great quote that might help me.

She said, "You can't boil the ocean."

I stood frozen, for a moment, and reflected on her sentence because it was extremely powerful. I have heard many quotes similar to that idea, such as, "Eat the elephant, one bite at a time" and "You can't simply do it all at once, so be sure and chunk it down to achieve your goal." You get the idea.

Perhaps it was my current, negative, frustrated state or the extra mimosa that really helped me marinate on this, but I was so perplexed and felt like I was standing frozen in time, to let that quote—"You can't boil the ocean"— sink in. Or perhaps it was one of those moments where you just needed to hear the same thing over and over again before you finally got it. (Moms everywhere get this one.)

Sometimes, it just takes a different way of saying the words for things to make sense. Perhaps I simply needed a different person to say those words to me, I'm not quite sure. Either way, that day, clarity hit me like a pile of bricks.

All day, I thought about what a genius statement that was, and wondered why we humans metaphorically attempt to boil the ocean.

We tend to see problems as so much bigger in our minds. We conjure up the worst-case scenarios. We make-believe we are faced with the utmost and biggest challenges that we can't fix or overcome. Yet, if we can't boil the ocean, why not think of them in smaller doses?

Why not only focus on what we can control? That is where change begins to happen. Being in control brings on a new level of confidence. You'll bring less stress into your life. You'll be less of a worrywart. If you get easily overwhelmed by tasks and projects, it is important to stay focused on the small, tiny, minute things that you can control, so you can keep moving forward, in a positive direction. As a result, I have learned to take action every day! My advice, therefore, is do something—anything. Even if it's the smallest of tasks, take action. It's all about progression, not perfection.

Then, celebrate those tiny victories, when you get them.

When things seem to be a bit too much, when you're in over your head, when you're scared or feeling like you're lost, or have those moments when you can't make sense of which way is up, one way to quickly stop that train of negative thought going 90 miles an hour in your head is to focus on gratitude. Gratitude is the recipe for changing your mindset. I've said it already in this book, but the more you focus on something, the more of that thing will keep showing up in your life. So, if you need to switch your focus and fast, do it with gratitude. You'll be amazed at how quickly you will begin to feel better. Your mind will be more at ease. Your body and demeanor will become more relaxed.

So, when the world seems to be lost, and all hope is gone, just remember you can't boil the ocean. What you can boil is a cup of tea. So, put the kettle on and start being grateful for everything in your life. This will help you to feel better, to change your state of mind to a more positive one, and it will help you think about how to overcome that roadblock that used to be a dead end.

CHAPTER 11 IN A NUTSHELL...

- Life is hard and we all face challenges, but you can overcome them if you adopt a "no dead end" mentality.
- Celebrate your tiny wins in big ways.
- You're working on progression, not perfection. Remember, perfection is the enemy of production.
- You can't boil the ocean, so stop trying to. Break things up into smaller, more achievable tasks or goals.
- Practice gratitude.

12

Grit and Determination

"Grit is living life like it's a marathon, not a sprint."

—*ANGELA LEE DUCKWORTH*

Most resourceful people have high levels of determination and grit. Some people may have what can be classified as stubbornness, but for the sake of this personal development book, I'll replace the word "stubbornness" with "grit."

Some people just seem to have it in them to endure the pain or "embrace the suck," to excruciating lengths. I know from personal experience that it takes a special uniqueness to hang in there when the going really gets tough.

But where does someone find the strength to keep persevering through more and more challenges?

1. Find the Little Wins

For starters, you can look for little wins. Normally, if I see someone who is typically very good at what they do, but they have had an "off" week or can't seem to move past something holding them back, I tell them to find a little win. That's it! Identify one little thing that you could be proud of; one little thing that you can say was a success during that particular day or week.

One little win will lead to another little win, then another, then another. The process becomes like building blocks, which lead you (and your brain) back to feeling like you can achieve your goals—or at least handle any other setbacks.

2. Laugh Out Loud

Literally. Another option is to laugh out loud. Seriously - This really works!

When you're at your lowest point, when the world seems to be at its worst, and all of a sudden, you get hit with bad news—the last and final punch to the gut—it really helps if you make light of the situation. It is true that when you're at the bottom, the only way to go is up. However, most people don't go up, they choose to stay stuck at the bottom, for extended periods of time. I assure you that if you attempt *anything*, it's only going to improve the scenario in a positive way, because the only way to go is up. One simple way to go up is by improving your mood.

I remember a clip from a Steve Carell movie (I can't remember the name; it was one of his unpopular flicks and I don't think it did very well), where he played a depressed, always down-in-the-dumps kind of character. One day, he was having one of those days where nothing seemed to be going his way. In the scene, he gets pulled over for speeding.

As the officer is writing him the ticket, his only reply is "Just add it to my tab." In a light-hearted, somewhat humorous way, that was like saying, "What else have you got? Just add it to my tab."

Sometimes, life can be really crappy, but if you can approach the crappy situation with a little humor, it ultimately can help you get through those moments.

3. Find the Happy Medium

Throughout my life, I've heard some pretty good advice from many people. One that seems to always get regurgitated is the advice of not getting too high on your highs or too low on your lows. You have to stay in that "Goldilocks" zone of just the right amount of highs and lows. Whether you are reflecting on the lessons or celebrating the accomplishments, the moment is short-lived.

You're in a constant motion of progression, keep moving, and stay grounded.

4. Become Self-Aware

When you find yourself looking for more willpower, the key that will help you is being self-aware. You have strengths and you have weaknesses (we all do), and if you are aware of your weaknesses, that will help you predict where you're going to get caught up or where you might veer off from your path to success. Being aware will enable you to predict those hurdles ahead of time.

Self-awareness is a process to learning and uncovering yourself, as a whole. Once you have reached a certain level of self-awareness, you'll see a huge improvement in your life. There will be improvement in your relationships, in your actions and behaviors, in your finances, in your health, and in many other key areas. You have areas that you will gravitate toward because it naturally makes sense for you and you're drawn to them or feel called and fulfilled by them. Yet, there will be other things that are a real struggle in areas you don't like, but are 100% necessary for you to do, or that you're not particularly passionate about, but you are going to have to do anyway. This is where your level of grit or determination will really serve you.

Once you've identified those problematic areas or tasks, you'll have to put your head down and just plow forward. It's like having to swallow medicine that tastes bad, or ripping a bandage off in a fast motion—it is best to get it over and done with. That is, by far, the best method to approach doing unwanted things. However, when it comes to your goals and striving for what you're passionate about in life, in becoming who you need to be in order to accomplish what you've set out to be, the tearing off of the bandage might take years, so you must keep your eye on the prize, the end result. Go back to your incredibly motivating *why*. Remember, you've come this far, there is no point in stopping now; you must continue the journey. Remember that you aren't looking for a final destination; you are looking for the next destination.

Growth is continuous, and when you achieve one goal, you'll need to set your sights on the next one that lies ahead.

Focus on getting to the next destination. Celebrate your unwavering tenacity and quickly move on to the area that you are most passionate about. It would be naive to think that the path to achieving a goal or becoming successful is smooth and easy.

As stated previously in this book, growth is messy and ugly. However, what you learn and what you gain from the messy stuff is what allows you then to achieve at a higher level. That ugly mess is what molds you into the resourceful person you are capable of being, who can overcome and surpass the challenges where others get hung up.

Growth and development are going to require a lot of grit and determination, so I have made a list of tips for how to prepare yourself to get through those tough or unfavorable tasks that you will need to complete.

How to Push Through, When You're in a Tough Spot:

1. **Seek Motivational Guidance**—This is important, at all times. Keep positive affirmations on sticky notes on your mirror—quick little words of inspiration you can find on Instagram or famous quotes by your mentors. Listen to podcasts that will inspire you. Thumb through past journal entries. Create and frequently look at a vision board or dream board. All these tools have to be at the ready to kick any doubts

out of your head and keep you ignited for moving toward your bigger life vision.

2. **Embrace Being the Underdog**—If life gets you down, instead of going into "victim mode," saying that your life is all over, remember the underdog. Everyone loves a good underdog story about the misfits everyone underestimated and all the ones no one first paid attention. That's a powerful role to have at your disposal. So, when you're caught up in the mess, embrace being the underdog. Embrace that people might be laughing at you right now, and embrace the fact that everyone you know is betting on you to fail. Not a soul thinks you'll stand a chance, which just means that when you go out swinging, they will all be noticing or admiring you, wondering how you did it and how you succeeded. When it feels like no one is supporting you, embrace being the underestimated underdog. It will give you power like you've never experienced.

3. **Dare to be Different**—This is what works for me. If I'm working toward something and I'm over halfway through it and feel like giving up, I remember this is where 80-90%

of my peers fell short. I don't like being like everyone else, and I don't like being lumped together with other average people, especially unmotivated, "all talk, no walk" kinds of people. So, when I think about quitting or giving up, I tell myself this is where the ones who are different *become* different. This is where the line in the sand is drawn, so to speak. This is where I get to the next level. Avoid proclaiming the same old New Year's resolutions that you didn't do a thing to achieve the year before. Tell yourself, *This is the moment I have been building up to. Everything, until now, was a bit easier.* This is why everyone was still in the running with you; it didn't get difficult until now. The difficult moments show up when you're over halfway through something. If you're anything like me and you don't want to be average, mediocre, and don't want to settle, then don't do what all the average, mediocre, people who settle do. They quit. You persevere. They complain. You encourage. They give up. You fight.

Believe me, I know the struggle is real. This is where motivation starts to die, because when you're in the middle of some terrible experience, it always looks and feels a lot like failure. So, it's harder to get back on the horse again. Yet, if you make it through this one hiccup, you're going to finish all the way. You're not tested at the 99% mark, or at the very end. You're tested three-fourths of the way through, at the 75% completion mark.

When you know there is still an exit ramp that you can take, your mind will tell you to consider taking it, but you must remember that what you've done and accomplished thus far isn't even close to what your true potential is. This is where you must maintain an unwavering focus on your goal and the desired outcome. So, harness the grit and the ability to persevere, because when you do, you'll be on your way to achieving great things.

CHAPTER 12 IN A NUTSHELL...

- When you're in the middle and everything around you looks and feels like failure, keep going.
- You will get off-course and sidetracked, but don't give up!
- What you've done and accomplished thus far isn't even close to what your true potential is, so keep pushing through.
- It's okay to be the underdog. People underestimating you could be your biggest motivation.

13

Discipline

"Discipline is the bridge between goals and accomplishments."

—JIM ROHN

As a society today, I believe we have misunderstood the word "discipline." If you use words in your vocabulary like "freedom," "flexibility," and "independence," the one word that conflicts with them in our minds is discipline. How can one be both flexible and disciplined? It sounds like an oxymoron, right? I was one of those people, in my twenties, although my young, stubborn and crazy self didn't want to believe it. Once I had a few more life experiences, I realized that being disciplined is actually the key to achieving freedom. It's the key to having more choices.

The idea that discipline would provide me with more freedom and flexibility in my life than not being disciplined was a huge idea for my mind to grasp. I believe that's why it took me so long to comprehend it. If you haven't lived through an experience like that where you can relate and say something like, "Yes, seven years ago, I learned that lesson, too," you might be very skeptical and you will remain skeptical until you see it through your own eyes or experience it yourself. That's okay. That's why learning to be resourceful is teachable!

Incorporating your disciplined habits will take time. Over time, you won't have to think about much because you will have created a conditioned response to a certain situation. The good news is you don't have to be disciplined in every single area of your life, just a few key areas—the areas that are paramount to your end goal. Start by understanding that success will require discipline, mostly in areas you aren't excited about. This is why success is hard. You have to be willing to do what the unsuccessful aren't—the difficult things. It's easy to give up or throw in the towel and justify your excuses.

Discipline requires that you create a conditioned response to a certain action, even if doing the action will suck or even if it is something you absolutely despise doing. Successful people will do it anyway, while someone who is inconsistent or undisciplined may give in.

When you don't allow yourself an exit ramp, your body will automatically implement what you have established. You establish it by practicing the disciplined habit.

The unique thing about discipline is that the more you have it, the easier and simpler your life will actually get. Most people have a negative association with the word "discipline." We tend to think that being disciplined means being a grumpy old fart who doesn't laugh at jokes or enjoy indulgences. For fun, let's play a game. I want you to close your eyes and picture a disciplined person. Who is the first one that pops in your head? Is it your demanding grade-school teacher, Mrs. Watson? A picture of Hitler, in full uniform? The grumpy old neighbor who always had something to say about your bike being left in his driveway? A strict librarian, always shushing those being too loud? I used to have these images in mind before, too.

After realizing that being disciplined is more a matter of being purposeful, controlled, and systematic, I began to see different images and people associated with the word. This goes back to the idea of programming I spoke about in the very first chapter. We've been programmed by society to believe that the word "discipline" (or those who are disciplined) has negative, unpleasant expressions or connotations. In reality, discipline is the key to unlocking your success.

I can be a carefree, spontaneous spirit, at times, so I had to change my emotions and thoughts around the word "discipline." I had to change my thinking toward this and other words, so that I could respond positively to it and them—words like "purposeful" and "controlled." Instead of creating a disciplined morning routine, I have a very controlled morning routine that allows me to accomplish what I need to accomplish for myself and my family. That small tweak in language made a huge difference for me.

I then started to evaluate my level of discipline. As it turned out, I didn't have a very high level of it in my life. I was only disciplined when something was easy or came naturally to me. If it was the least bit challenging, I used to create a story as to why it wasn't something I was interested in. I later discovered that being disciplined is what successful people thrive at in order to achieve what they want to achieve. This is not to say that disciplined people don't have fun or laugh or find joy in life. Rather, it's the opposite—being disciplined in the right areas of their lives catapults them to success and allows them the options of whatever it is they choose!

I am now happy to report that I have a very purposeful schedule for exercising so I'm not wasting an hour, pretending to work out. I now use planning tools to map out my most important goals and to-do items each week. These seem like small areas to be disciplined in, yet it's what leads to a bigger life. Being disciplined in the right areas and for the right amount of time can impact your life tremendously. Even though you will get the thoughts that creep in and tell you, "Sleep in, it's just one day," "You don't *have to* go to the gym," or "One sleeve of Oreos won't kill you," you have to push through those weak moments and be disciplined enough to say "No" or be disciplined enough that if you do fall off the wagon, you are able to jump right back on.

So, let's try this again. Close your eyes and picture someone you admire who is successful. Picture someone who is passionate, purposeful, and controlled. Who comes to mind? What's their level of discipline around the way in which they lead their lives? How much control do they have with how they spend their time? Think about Tony Robbins, Darren Hardy, John Maxwell, Rachel Hollis, Sara Blakely, Jeff Bezos, and Hal Elrod. See their excellence as an example of possibilities for you.

Do you now have a different emotion or feel positive when you hear the word "discipline"? I sure hope so! Be sure to strengthen those positive emotions and associations with the word "discipline," because it is through having discipline that will unlock a world of possibilities for you and your goals. The best and most resourceful people know that being disciplined leads to success.

CHAPTER 13 IN A NUTSHELL...

- Make sure you have a positive association with the word "discipline."
- Incorporating your disciplined habits will take time.
- Think of other passionate, purposeful, and controlled people to help you enjoy being a disciplined person.
- Discipline = Freedom.

14

Find Inspiration

"There is no heavier burden than an unfulfilled potential."

—*CHARLES SCHULZ*

Look for inspiration.

I've found the best place to find inspiration is through the people who have gone before you. Think about it. You're not the first. (That should be a relief for you to hear.) You're not the first person to want to achieve success. You're not the first person to have a huge desire inside of them, to want to conquer their fears, to throw caution to the wind, or to make an exciting change toward a better future.

You can learn from those who've gone before you, those who have figured out the way to deal or adjust to challenges, those that think big, those who ask powerful questions, and those who have high levels of resourcefulness. They will become your new best friends. Study them! Study their behaviors and their actions. Know their stories of failure and learn from them so you can quicken your own growth path. Note the scenarios to avoid or pitfalls that cause things to not work out. Catalog all the wins and successful things that moved them toward their end goal. You will then have a system to follow that will lead you where you'd like to be. You'll have a mentor, or a tour guide, so to speak, that you can mimic. You can do this with anyone! Look at a few from the following list, who most people are familiar with: Darren Hardy, Gary Vaynerchuk, Sarah Blakely, Oprah, Richard Branson, Warren Buffet, Rachel Hollis, Simon Sinek, Steve Jobs, and Tony Robbins. Look at athletes like Mike Jordan, Wayne Gretzky, or Tiger Woods. The list goes on and on. The world is not short of any amazing role models to follow and learn from.

Success stories of others are a great way for you to learn—from their lessons and mistakes, instead of your own—so you won't have to waste all your time going through trial and error to figure out your next move. Plus, if you want to achieve success and become a successful person, you need to do what other successful people have done—with your own spin, of course, with your passion and your own personal touch.

For the most part, there are tons of common denominators that successful people have or things that they do that makes them who they are! For example, if you study the habits of a few of these folks, you will find similarities such as what time they wake up in the morning, what they do in their spare time, and how they prepare for a busy week or the day ahead. What I have found is that they all wake up extremely early, they all are able to put themselves first, their health is almost always a priority, they are laser-focused on their visions and what they are working toward, and their time is carefully calculated to be the most purposeful as possible. As for their spare time, the majority of them read books, educate themselves further, and travel. Traveling is the perfect teacher. You will learn a way more from your experiences firsthand, rather than from a Netflix original. Another big thing I've noticed is that they all provide value to others, whether it's through teaching, the books they write, or the people they know and expose the world to. Every single one provides something others will value.

It's important to take notes on what the common themes are among great people. It's also important to note that they didn't all have the same circumstances, they didn't all grow up the same, and they weren't all given the same opportunities. Yet they all have created a limitless life—growing to their best potential, day in and day out—and they all aspire to become their best version of themselves.

Start following some of these folks on Instagram, sign up for their e-newsletters, and/or take some of their training courses. Any of those things will help catapult you forward to your desired future outcomes. You can simply use Google to find more people amongst these greats and find more inspiring stories. Pick one or a few that resonate most with you and your story. Find the one that inspires you and ignites that passion you have for your own success, and use them to harness your resourcefulness and create the life you deserve.

CHAPTER 14 IN A NUTSHELL...

- Look to others for inspiration—especially successful people who have come before you.
- Find some mentors to follow and study their behaviors and their actions.
- Study the resourcefulness and success of who you want to become and learn from them

15

Get a Coach

"A coach is someone who tells you what you don't want to hear, who has you see what you don't want to see, so you can be who you have always known you could be."

—*TOM LANDRY*

What do athletes and other successful people in their industries have in common? Yes, they are elitists in their professions. Most likely, they all are pretty similar with their habits and work ethics. They all work extremely hard to practice, improve, and get better, yet what's really interesting is that each has a coach.

Some of the greatest athletes of all time have coaches. Grammy-winning singers have vocal coaches. And resourceful, smart, and successful business people also have coaches!

In this chapter, it's important to know that being coachable is a skill set you've obtained by becoming resourceful, which coincides with also having a coach. That's just simple logic—how can you be coachable without someone coaching you, right? I intentionally used the word "coach," not because the word "coachable" has coach in it, but because having a coach is what makes the difference. It's not the same as having a mentor you look up to, or having a consultant tell you what to do. Think about it, for a minute. Have you ever noticed that words like "mentor-able" or "consultant-able" aren't even real words? You'll find "mentored" or "consulted" (the past tenses of "mentor" and "consult") in the dictionary, but the only word that exists with a definition in the present, actionable tense is the word "coachable." Mentors are great connections to have, and a consultant could come in handy, sure, should you need precise direction on a topic, but a coach is different. A coach is a partner.

Coaches have the same goals as you do. They have the same risks and the same things at stake as you do. That's what creates the unique relationship and leads to successful results.

Think about it again, from a sports perspective. When a team wins a championship, doesn't the coach also win? With all the sports awards athletes receive, coaches receive athletic awards, too. There is "Coach of the Year," "Legendary coach," and many more. I know they get those Super Bowl rings, too. The coaches show up at all the practices, not just on game days. They are there in the "off season," training and working to grow talent for their organizations (just think about any of the professional drafts we have, or the college recruiting process—it's intense!).

Coaching is a year-round responsibility. It is an all-encompassing job.

Coaches are one with their team and players. A great visual for this is baseball. I never quite understood why, but a baseball coach actually wears the team's uniform. That's sort of odd, yet isn't it a great picture of unity? Coach and players on the same level!

In business, it's the same thing. A coach is on the frontline of their client's business. Their goals are their client's goals. A good coach will interrogate your level of commitment by incorporating some accountability. They will also keep you in "action mode," because they are a partner with their clients. That's what makes having a coach different.

A coach will help you see your actions through to a result. Setting goals and casting a vision is only part of the equation. You need to stay in "action mode," in order to keep doing things, so you can see the results you desire. By having a coach, you will begin to see all the potential inside of you. You will create a new community of other like-minded, goal-driven people. With a coach, you will have better clarity as to what to focus on and what action steps are most important for you. You will have a detailed plan; a roadmap; a strong, foundational blueprint. Having a coach will allow you to make wise decisions, keep you aware of your blind spots, and bring you to a whole new level!

So, get into action—massive action—by hiring a good coach. (There are great coaching tools in the back of this book, in the Resources section.)

If you don't act, everything you've invested in up until now is simply a waste—a waste of time, a waste of money, and a waste of resources—because the thing we are all searching for or measuring to see is results.

If we have no results, how do we know if what we are doing is working and worth repeating? How do we know whether to continue or cease? How do we know whether or not to add more investments of time or money, or to simply put those resources to use in another way?

Results give us those answers and bring us to focus on the next steps. Remember, we only get results by taking actions.

We only get to reflect and evaluate *after* we attempt something. If we don't see ourselves moving toward where we desire to be, then it's simply a waste.

Taking action is critical and a coach is there to help you with those actions every step of the way.

CHAPTER 15 IN A NUTSHELL...

- Hire a coach! Get someone in your world who cares enough about you to push you, keep you focused, and remind you of your *why*.
- No one succeeds alone—no one!
- Resourceful people are coachable.
- Taking action is critical and a coach is there to help you with those actions every step of the way.

Part 4: CONCLUSION—Figuring it Out!

So, here it is—your chance to begin, to start your own personal development journey toward becoming resourceful, and for you to devote time to learning the skills and creating the habits that will lead to your future success as well as the very best version of yourself.

You are now armed with what all the other successful people who have gone before you are armed with. All you need to do is stay committed to your success. The only thing that could possibly stand in your way is *you,* so be sure to think like a resourceful person.

Implement the habits and operations of a resourceful person. Have the grit and tenacity of a resourceful person. Then, there's really no stopping you! It's important to remember this is all about what you desire your life to be.

This is your life and you are in complete control of your future. The only way to create the life that makes you happy is to keep that vision of your greatest life in your mind—not other people's expectations of you, or what they want for you, or what they think is best for you. You have to let all those go. Release all those expectations, those self-imposed limiting beliefs, and trade them in for the life you deserve to be living, to demonstrate for your children and grandchildren a life of possibilities; a life of abundance.

Demonstrate that being and acting resourceful will get you far in this life, that being resourceful can open up more chances for you, create more opportunities for you, and help you overcome challenges and/or obstacles that others can't seem to figure out.

Opportunity is out there! It's yours for the taking. Once you believe that, anything is possible. Then take immediate, massive action toward your goals. When you do that, you'll have catapulted your life toward achieving success.

You now know the tools and skills that successful people possess. What's even better is that you now have a roadmap to achieving those same skill sets, to help you on your own journey toward the life you deserve and were meant to live.

Remember, being ordinary won't get you to the top. You have to stand out! Harness your newfound skills to be more resourceful and take over the driver's seat of your life.

Don't be a spectator. Don't let the great moments pass you by. That's no way to live your life to the fullest.

It's important to live with intention, to live with passion, and to live each day by being resourceful.

You can now dedicate the next part of your life to making sure you become a more resourceful person, because resourceful people become successful people by simply figuring it out!

Questions for You

"Life is a question, and how we live it is our answer. How we phrase the questions we ask ourselves determines the answer that eventually become our life"

—*From the book,* The ONE Thing

What is one mistake you've made that has led to your new understanding or new belief?

What's next for you?

Who are some of your mentors? Who do you admire?

In what ways are you learning?

What is an area of expertise for you?

What questions did I not ask that you would have liked me to ask?

What would you do and love every day, even if you were failing at it?

How can you use your talents to help others?

FIGURE IT OUT

What kind of experience would you have to create for your consumer to defend you against your competitor?

Are you clinging to the problem or embracing the solution?

In what ways can you add more value?

What did you learn today that will help you grow?

What do you desire your legacy to be?

What are you doing today to become the person you want to be?

Because our struggles determine our success, what are you willing to struggle for?

Did you lead by example today?

Are you rejecting the limitations of common thinking in order to accomplish uncommon results?

What does success mean to you?

What do you want to be known for?

Are your actions in alignment with your expectations?

You become what you think about, so what are you becoming?

What creates stress in your life? How can you eliminate it?

Are you taking responsibility for your thoughts, words, and actions, on a daily basis?

How are your fears getting in the way of your goals?

What other options can you create? What are possible solutions?

What have you accomplished that you're most proud of?

How does this relate to your life purpose?

What are you currently treating like a priority that is actually a distraction?

What are you discovering about the way you think?

What is one thing you can say "no" to, in order to ensure success?

Recommended Reads

Mindset, Personal Development & Self-Help

The 12 Week Year by Brian Moran

Start with Why: How Great Leaders Inspire Everyone to Take Action by Simon Sinek

Miracle Morning by Hal Elrod

Atomic Habits by James Clear

The ONE Thing by Gary Keller and Jay Papasan

Grit by Angela Duckworth

Write it Down, Make it Happen by Henriette Anne Klauser

The Road Less Stupid by Keith Cunningham

How Successful People Think by John Maxwell

Emotional Intelligence 2.0 by Travis Bradberry and Jean Greaves

The Compound Effect by Darren Hardy

The Passion Test by Janet Attwood

Financial

6 Steps to 7 Figures by Pat Hiban

Set for Life by Scott Trench

Wealth Can't Wait by David Osborn

You Are a BadAss at Making Money by Jen Sincero

Profit First by Mike Michalowicz

The Simple Path to Wealth by JL Collins

Business and Leadership

Culture Wins by William Vanderbloemen

Principles by Ray Dalio

Traction by Gino Wickman

First, Break all the Rules: What the World's Greatest Managers Do Differently by Jim Harter

Outliers by Malcolm Gladwell

First, Fast, Fearless: How to Lead Like a Navy SEAL by Brian Hines

The Ultimate Blueprint for an Insanely Successful Business by Keith Cunningham

Good Leaders Ask Great Questions by John Maxwell

Dare to Lead by Brené Brown

Scale: Seven Proven Principles to Grow Your Business and Get Your Life Back by Jeff Hoffman and David Finkel

The Great Game of Business by Jack Stack

The New One Minute Manager by Ken Blanchard

The Five Dysfunctions of a Team: A Leadership Fable by Patrick Lencioni

People and Relationships

7L: The Seven Levels of Communication by Michael Mayer

The 5 Love Languages by Gary Chapman

StrengthsFinder 2.0 by Tom Rath

Fierce Conversations by Susan Scott

FIGURE IT OUT

Coaching Tools and Resources

Visit www.katemeiner.com for access to great coaching tools and freebies!

Some of the things you will find there are:

- A one-page Business Plan
- A one-page Goal-Setting Tool
- Access Hiring and HR Tools
- And MUCH More!

> You can also complete a FREE Business Assessment!

For more on coaching, contact me via email at kate@mymapscoach.com.

Connect with Me on Social Media

Facebook.com/bizcoachkate

Instagram @bizcoach_katemeiner and @katemeiner

Acknowledgements

To my friends and family—you have supported me and encouraged me throughout this process. I truly appreciate all the love and cheers you've sent my way.

To all of you from my KW family—there are far too many people to name individually, but know that I am grateful to be in business with each of you. It's sincerely an honor to know and experience such a tremendous group of high-level achievers who have shared this experience of personal growth and development alongside me.

To my coaches—throughout the process, I have had many coaches to help me stay focused and on track in pursuit of my goal of being an author. Thank you for continuously raising the standards and providing me with the courage to see it through. Sarah, Tim, and Scott, you guys rock! Thanks also to MJ for taking me under your wing and teaching me, encouraging me, and treating me like a daughter. You've had a major impact on what I thought was possible and I wouldn't be here today without your guidance and support. Thank you!

FIGURE IT OUT

To the SPS community—to all the fellow authors, students, and staff in the Self-Publishing School community, the great systems in the training and the overflow of support and guidance along the way has been amazing. Thank you to all who joined the launch team, brainstormed with me, and held me accountable. Finally, to my kick-ass author-chicks group—Michelle, Erin, and Danielle—you three are all so inspirational and I'm excited to be on this journey with you.

To my editor, Lorraine—This book would still be a presentation for a classroom versus being a book in the hands of readers. I'm so grateful you took a chance on me and allowed this book to reach so many people. Thank you for the improvements and for making this book better.

To all of you, the readers—for purchasing this book and for your passion to learn and grow to become more resourceful. Thank you for your support!

To my daughter Logan—you are, by far, the single most amazing thing in my life. The joy you bring lights up my entire world. May you continue to grow, laugh, dream big, and create the life you aspire to live. I love you and am so proud to be your mom.

About the Author

Kate Meiner is a Certified Business Coach, Author, and Speaker who has a personal mission to influence, inspire, and impact the lives of others. She led a successful Keller Williams brokerage, an organization of over 170 independent business owners, teaching the self-employed to think like business owners and run their businesses like businesses. She has a passion for coaching, training, and developing leaders in the business world so they can go out and leave their footprint in the marketplace.

Kate believes that resourcefulness is the most underrated skill in today's business environment—and one that is missing from most personal development teachings. *Figure it Out* teaches each reader the five foundational trait skills which are crucial in the journey to becoming a master of resourcefulness: Problem-solving, curiosity, adaptability, observation, and creativity.

Currently a resident of Central Florida, Kate is the proud mother of her beloved daughter, Logan, and has been married to her college sweetheart, Tim, since 2013. Her love for travel has fueled her passion for meeting exciting people, tasting great foods, and having new experiences all over the world. She also enjoys life's simple pleasures, such as time with family, coffee, wine, and baking.

For more information on Kate's books, coaching, keynote speaking, free resources, and more, visit her website at www.katemeiner.com. You can also follow Kate on Instagram at @bizcoach_katemeiner and @katemeiner.

www.ingramcontent.com/pod-product-compliance
Lightning Source LLC
Chambersburg PA
CBHW070149100426
42743CB00013B/2860